Dancing When the Lights Go Out

Overcoming Grief

Roger Greene

malcolm down
PUBLISHING

First published 2024 by Malcolm Down Publishing Ltd.
www.malcolmdown.co.uk

28 27 26 25 24   7 6 5 4 3 2 1

British Library Cataloguing in Publication Data
A catalogue record for this book is available from the British Library.

ISBN 978-1-915046-83-3

Cover design by Sarah Holloway.
Art direction by Sarah Grace.

Printed in the UK.

Typeset using Atomik ePublisher from Easypress Technologies.

This book is dedicated to the life of Vicky Greene.
Just one of her many legacies to the world.

You can't judge a book by looking at the cover
2015
The year Vicky was diagnosed with dementia

For those facing grief or trauma and for those giving care to those who grieve, this book is a Godsend. With a vulnerable and tender narrative, Roger Greene shares the story of his own pain-filled journey facing up to early dementia with his wife, Vicky, and then the double blow of her tragic death during COVID with no family members allowed to care or even to be present at the moment of death.

Roger challenges our notions of death and shares practical ways to handle and process grief, explains the difference between grief and mourning and gives accessible, practical, no-nonsense advice. That advice includes exactly how to talk to and engage with those who mourn, and with equal weight and helpfulness, explains how to best navigate the complex and sometimes unhelpful world of NHS, Social Services and care home funding and placement.

Every pastor or church leader should have this book on their shelf.

And for those that mourn, this book is one practical manifestation of the promised comfort.

David Oliver, author of **All About Heaven.**

Experiencing grief and loss is part of being human and yet we prepare little for it, especially in Western culture. Roger has articulated his own bereavement journey with stunning clarity. I'm in no way exaggerating when I say that this is an essential read. I don't say that lightly or glibly. I'll be recommending this widely because it will deeply help us all.

Carl Beech, CEO Edge Ministries, President of Christian Vision for Men (CVM), and founder of the men's festival The Gathering.

Roger is a true friend, wise counsel and inspiration. He has an ability to pinpoint problems, understand what is needed and then articulate a way through to a healthy, life-giving outcome. In a culture that struggles to deal with loss in life and in death, Roger wears his heart on his sleeve as he navigates the reader through his own personal story of losing his wife, Vicky, with transparent honesty and vulnerability.

Along the way his down-to-earth insights, discovered through pain and grief, give permission to the reader to face and work through their own loss, leading to hope and a positive future. This happened in me as I read through these pages over a few days. Roger unpacks the emotional and mental minefield of loss, giving practical advice to help understand and process what is happening in you, but not to get stuck there. His hope-filled story through the pain of loss inspires you to grieve well, enabling you to move forward into the next season of your life.

Clive Urquhart, senior pastor, Kingdom Faith Church, Horsham.

This book is an incredible tapestry of a deeply personal experience, thought provoking theology and highly practical wisdom around a subject we HAVE to talk about – death.

Roger's journey, in caring for his wife Vicky who was suffering dementia, is both eye-opening and heartbreaking. You will not read this without shedding many tears, and that is a good thing, because we all need to become aware of the impact and strain dementia has on the sufferer and the families involved.

The spiritual, emotional and practical value of this book is immeasurable, especially when studied with others using the questions provided at the end of each chapter.

Roger does not set out to minimise the impact of grief, in fact quite the opposite. He guides us in a conversation that leads to maximising the life we get to live today. I cannot recommend this book enough.

Gareth Morgan, elite performance coach and author of **The Winning Conversation** *and* **The Winning Keys.** *Leader of Everyday Champions Church UK.*

The Spirit of the Sovereign LORD is on me,
because the LORD has anointed me
to proclaim good news to the poor.
He has sent me to bind up the broken-hearted …
to comfort all who mourn,
and provide for those who grieve in Zion –
to bestow on them a crown of beauty
instead of ashes,
the oil of joy
instead of mourning,
and a garment of praise
instead of a spirit of despair.
They will be called oaks of righteousness,
a planting of the LORD
for the display of his splendour.

    (Isaiah 61:1-3)

Contents

Introduction

This is a story about finding hope and meaning in dark times and seemingly hopeless circumstances.

It is about being human and the pain of grief. It's about wrestling with faith amid unfathomable suffering. It is the story of my wife's death, way too young and cruelly separated from her family, with a lethal cocktail of dementia and COVID-19 at the height of a global pandemic.

It is about the battle in our minds and spirits as we journey through grievous loss, and how we can navigate the storms of life. It is about the choices we face and the choices we make.

It's also a story about how badly prepared I was to deal with her death, regardless of my faith and a long career working in and around healthcare.

God designed us human beings to live a mysterious dance of body, spirit and soul. This story is about the whole of our being, our minds, emotions, thoughts and the choices we make, as well as the mysterious and intangible stuff we call faith.

Loss and grief impact every level of our being. The journey is messy and can't be neatly packaged into the rational, the spiritual, the psychological, the emotional, the theoretical, the inexplicable or the practical. It's full of paradox, full of complex inter-connections. It isn't a linear and organised story with an easy pattern to tell or to follow. Yet we must start somewhere.

Like every other human being on the planet, I am a relational, emotional, rational, irrational, spiritual and hormonal bunch of contradictions wrapped up in a single skeleton and skin.

I live in a Western culture that has conditioned me to celebrate success and see life as a process of continuous improvement and smooth progression until I decide it's time to stop of my own volition.

The absurdity of that viewpoint is that I know life isn't like that. Harsh and brutal stuff happens that I don't want to happen, whether I like it or not.

It's a culture where I am conditioned to feel ashamed of failure as a waste of potential or opportunity. Or if I fail, it should be something or someone else's fault; I should be able to blame something or someone else. Think about it: even our medical language for death is failure – 'heart failure', 'kidney failure', 'pulmonary failure'.

Is it any surprise that we have difficulty relating genuinely to family and friends who have experienced grievous loss? If you are anything like me, you may know the bare outline and facts of what's happened, but often I haven't known what to say or do to help. We don't like to pry, do we? We don't want to upset people unnecessarily, do we? Or do we just feel helpless to help?

I have known of people crossing the street to avoid that awkward conversation with a relative who lost her husband. Sometimes it's easier to avoid the subject altogether for fear of upsetting someone.

To experience loss and grief is human. The simple truth is that loss and grief are unavoidable in life. That's not being pessimistic, it's not a lapse of faith, it's just realistic. And while my story is about a loss through premature death, I know grievous loss can also be caused by a divorce, the loss of a job, a home, a catastrophic health incident, a career, or a random accident. I'm not qualified to write about those things because I am fortunate not to have experienced them – but I know from conversations with friends and family who have experienced them just how deeply such losses affect their lives.

And just so you know your money has been well spent on this book, there is some practical stuff about the things I learned along the way, and the things I wish I had known in advance to prepare me to navigate the journey better.

Before this excruciating loss, I would never have been qualified to write about it.

I am not qualified as a professional expert in counselling, psychotherapy, psychiatry or any other of the multiple therapies that can be of such great help at times of loss. I am not a theologian capable of unravelling the unfathomable mysteries of God. I am, however, interested in all those fields of learning because they help me understand the human condition as a dance between body, spirit and soul. The whole person, just as God made us. For that reason, you will find me frequently referring to the work of psychologists and philosophers as well as biblical truth and revelation by the Holy Spirit.

I am qualified to write about loss through bereavement because I'm what is fashionably known as an 'expert by experience'. It's the experience of losing my wife, who was also mother to our children, a grandmother to our grandchildren, a sister to her siblings, an auntie to her nieces and nephews, a sister-in-law to my siblings, a woman of great faith and an inspirational and dearly loved friend to so many. And that makes me deeply qualified.

I have a second qualification which is simple curiosity about how we all behave around loss and grief. I knew intuitively that people who were close to me felt helpless and didn't know what to say or do. Yet others were able to step forward and gather around me, cook me a meal and deliver it unannounced, or offer to talk even if they couldn't be with me because of the COVID-19 pandemic lockdown rules in place at the time.

That curiosity led me to engage with friends and family about their experiences, and with professionals in the world of psychology and counselling about their perspectives. After all, professionals are not just qualified to help people, they are human too and have experienced personal loss and grief.

I am deeply thankful for all their contributions and wisdom that have enriched the insights in this book, so many of which guided me through a long and painful journey and out the other side to live in hope for the future on this earth as well as the next.

This story is my attempt to give this complex mess some meaning because:

- So much mental ill-health in our society is caused by a culture that treats death and loss as taboo subjects.
- We must talk openly about death and loss so we can live full and meaningful lives – after all, we are going to die someday and lose people we love, so we need to be prepared.
- A world in pain needs people who understand the reality and suffering of deep grief so as to restore hope to the soul with deep understanding and humanity.
- And of course, it has helped me process my own deep grief at the loss of my wife to dementia and her subsequent death from COVID-19.

I hope our story will explain some things. I trust it will help you find hope and meaning through the pain of loss. But above all, I trust it will help us to live our lives better by embracing more fully our fragile humanity, our spirituality and the inevitability of loss and death.

And although it is full of paradox and complexity, it is also remarkably simple in so many ways.

My experience has helped me explore more deeply what it means when Jesus said 'those who mourn' are 'blessed' (Matthew 5:4). I know what it means now to wear a 'garment of praise' instead of a 'spirit of despair' (Isaiah 61:3).

You will also notice my references to song lyrics throughout the book. Songwriters and poets get this stuff about our everyday lives and our humanity. Let's turn their poetry into the everyday language of life. That's what I mean about 'dancing when the lights go out'.[1]

I hope it can help you in your journey through life. I hope it can help us collectively to see death and celebrate life differently, with greater realism, more hope, and less fear.

I hope it can help us be a light to a world in pain.

Let's talk about death so we can live.

---

1 'Everyday Life' written by Chris Martin, Guy Berryman, John Metcalfe, Jonathan Buckland and Will Champion. Copyright © 2019 Universal Music Publishing MGB Ltd and Copyright Control. All rights reserved.

Chapter One: Finding Love

She was the young woman who stood out in the crowd at the busy cross-roads as I gazed out from the top deck of the bus. She was stunning, dressed in her hippy-style Afghan coat, bright yellow polo-neck sweater, black jeans, long and flowing dark hair and radiant face. One in a million.

Two days later at the same time, I spotted her again from the top deck of the bus. I just hoped she was walking down to the university campus where I might get a chance to see her among the thousands of other students.

I was captivated by the beauty of a young woman I hadn't met. She was already occupying my thoughts and daydreams but felt like some unreachable ideal.

The next day I mistakenly walked into the wrong classroom for my tutorial. As I opened the door, all eyes turned towards me like some intruder into their world... including hers. Our eyes met. I knew she had seen me.

My dreamlike ideal of this young woman was not only real, but she was in the same Modern Languages department as me.

We were in the same university department, but in different years. I was in my final year, and she was in her first year. Our timetables were completely different, and we had different groups of friends. At best, she would be coming out of a lecture or a tutorial at the same time as I was going into one, meaning the opportunity never came to hang around in the lobby between classes and casually say hello or try some corny chat-up line that I would doubtless stumble over, wince and regret.

It was also clear that she had already attracted a strong cluster of male and female friends, so she was never alone, never without at least one male companion by her side.

About a month into the term my friend Jerry decided to produce a Brazilian play and asked me to take the lead role. The plan was to perform the drama at a residential weekend before Christmas. I was invited along to rehearse one Sunday afternoon.

And there she was. Only this time her male bodyguards were not there. We all introduced ourselves to the group. I discovered she was Vicky, but with a foreign-sounding surname I couldn't instantly recognise or remember but turned out to be Wratislaw. She was fluent in Portuguese and had been brought up in Angola until the age of seventeen, despite the Eastern European surname.

I had so idealised her that I could not approach or speak to her. But as all good producers do, Jerry made all the prospective members of the cast connect with each other. I was tongue-tied like a nervous teenager who didn't want his dreams shattered by rejection and doubtless saying something stupid, if anything at all. But at least we were now in the same room, in the same production and the rehearsals were only just starting. I knew I would get the chance to see her again at least every Sunday afternoon for the next couple of months, even if I fluffed my lines with her now.

It still felt like a bubble of unreality where I was suddenly face to face with the one-in-a-million young woman I had glimpsed from the top of the bus.

After several rehearsals, I plucked up the courage to invite her out on a date to see a film. She told me she would love to, but she had a headache. My heart sank. She insisted, however, that she wasn't just giving me the classic blow-off line, but she really did have a migraine.

I persisted and one day after rehearsals she accepted an invitation to go to a party with me the following weekend. I had played rugby in the afternoon and turned down the routine invitation to the pub after the game so I could get ready to pick her up. I arrived at her flat at the appointed time, where I was greeted by a flatmate who told me that she had gone to London with a male friend to see a karate exhibition. Her flatmate told me Vicky had tried to ring me, but back in the day we had no mobile phones, no emails, no messaging and only one payphone per student residence. And apparently no one had answered the phone where I lived.

I was now convinced I was being strung along. I had been stood up. I was done. Enough was enough.

The following day there was a knock on my door to say there was someone on the phone. It was Vicky. She was deeply apologetic for standing me up and said she had gone to London as a last-minute opportunity as she so loved karate and couldn't bear to miss the exhibition. She knew the guy she had gone with fancied her, but she reassured me that the feeling was not mutual. And she asked if my invitation was still open to get together?

And that's how our love affair began.

Forty years, three daughters and three grandchildren later, I drove her to an outpatient appointment with a consultant psychiatrist who specialised in memory loss.

She had reluctantly agreed to see her GP a year earlier at the insistence of her family because of notable changes in her character and an increase in obsessive behaviours that were accompanied by a dramatic loss of social inhibition. She didn't think there was anything wrong but went along to keep us all quiet.

A year's worth of appointments with a psychiatrist made little difference. His prescription of antidepressants had no effect, primarily because she refused to renew the prescription. He was unable to diagnose any underlying psychosis or mental illness, and so he referred her for an MRI scan of the brain, and to a colleague who specialised in memory loss.

And that's how we came to be sitting together in the consulting room of a psychiatrist who specialised in memory loss on 15 December 2015. The date is etched deep in my memory.

The psychiatrist asked Vicky a range of questions that she was unable to answer. She then spoke with Vicky about her concerns for her memory. She had also read the reports from her consultant psychiatrist colleague and a consultant radiologist about the MRI scan results.

She told us as gently as she could that she thought Vicky had possibly contracted a rare type of dementia called frontotemporal dementia, affecting people between the ages of forty-five and sixty-five. If that was the case, she told us it was untreatable. There was no medication either to cure or alleviate such a condition.

It was clear that Vicky did not understand what the consultant was saying and had no insight into the implications for her future. The only thing she really understood was that this lady was telling her that she was not allowed to drive her car anymore, and she really didn't like that.

In those few minutes my world fell apart. I was stunned. My deepest fear had just come true. I was tongue-tied again, only this time because I was speechless in a dream-like bubble of unreality.

Vicky was a very young sixty-one. How could it be possible that my beautiful, creative, passionate and compassionate wife now had an untreatable, degenerative brain disease? I had thought that only happened to people in their eighties and nineties. But surely not Vicky?

I had been holding on to the hope that her condition was treatable, and our lives were just on pause. When Vicky was better, we would resume our normal lives, wouldn't we?

Now I was being told that all that hope was gone and our plans for the future had evaporated. The dream I dared to imagine forty years earlier on the upper deck of a bus had now turned to a nightmare.

In her letter to Vicky's GP, the consultant later described my reaction in the classically understated way doctors do, as 'teary'. I wasn't teary. I was completely and utterly wrecked.

But my job now was to pull myself together and help her live her life as fully and well as she could. Those fateful minutes in the consulting room had transformed me from husband to carer. They had changed both Vicky's and my life forever.

Three and a half years later I had to accept that caring for Vicky at home wasn't safe for either of us. I had to entrust her into the hands of professionals in a dementia care home. I felt guilty that I was abandoning her without her knowledge or consent. I was overwhelmed by the sense that I was breaking our marriage covenant. Deep inside I knew that she would never return to the home that she had lovingly created for our family, and where she had exercised so well her great gift of hospitality.

So great was the impact of her care home admission that after just thirty-six hours she no longer knew who I was. I felt wrecked again – and not for the last time.

In April 2020, eight months after her admission to her third and final care home, I received a call from the manager asking my consent to test Vicky for COVID-19 as she was clearly unable to consent for herself. We now had to face a new and frightening reality that she had contracted COVID-19 in the first wave of the first year of the global pandemic. It was six weeks since the national imposition of a lockdown on care homes, so neither I nor any other member of our family had seen her during that period because of the strict prohibition of visitors under any circumstances, not even spouses or children.

Eleven days later, I received a call from the nurse on duty telling me Vicky had lost consciousness for a few minutes after her lunch, but she had recovered. Before we could finish the conversation, the nurse excused herself to attend to an urgent matter.

When I rang back ten minutes later, she told me she was so sorry – but Vicky had just died. And then she informed me that, because of the lockdown rules, I could not even go to see her or be with her.

Losing my wife was painful enough. Losing her when I wasn't permitted to see her for seven weeks before she died, to hold her hand or to be with her when she breathed her last breath, felt inhumane. That the prevailing law of the land meant my family and friends couldn't mourn her death or celebrate her life together just compounded the depth of our sorrow and pain. It multiplied our sense of loss. And I felt as though I had failed her again. Guilt kicked in, as well as deep sorrow. My emotions went into overdrive.

My mourning did not feel like a blessing. These were dark times for me and my family.

Chapter Two: Dealing with Dark Times

Blessed are those who mourn,
for they will be comforted.
   (Matthew 5:4)

My mourning after Vicky's death didn't feel like blessing. What Jesus said in the Sermon on the Mount was one of those Scripture verses I had accepted blindly as another of his countercultural teachings without ever processing what he really meant. But now I realise I had to go through deep mourning to understand.

During the later years of the journey through Vicky's decline with dementia, I listened constantly to worship music through my headphones when out walking, or a Bluetooth speaker I carried from room to room at home. The worship kept me connected to God through our painful journey. The worship didn't change the circumstances, but it changed how I felt and kept me anchored in hope. It was like God gave me a new song at each stage of the journey, weaving me a 'garment of praise' (Isaiah 61:3) to replace my despair.

'In Over My Head'[2] by Bethel Music was one of those songs at the time I felt most overwhelmed and helpless:

And you crash over me.
And that's where you want me to be.
I'm going under, I'm in over my head.
Whether I sink, whether I swim.
It makes no difference when I'm beautifully in over my head.

Deep grief had made me feel out of control, and I really felt way in over my

---

2 'In Over My Head (Crash Over Me)' written by Jenn Johnson and John-Paul Gentile. Copyright © 2014 Bethel Music Publishing. All rights reserved.

head. How could I be 'beautifully in over my head' in my grief? It seemed such a paradox. That word again.

After Vicky died, I heard a sermon called 'How to Deal with Dark Times'[3] by the late Dr Tim Keller, where he quotes Psalm 88:15-18:

> From my youth I have suffered and been close to death; I have borne your terrors and am in despair. Your wrath has swept over me; your terrors have destroyed me. All day long they surround me like a flood; they have completely engulfed me. You have taken from me friend and neighbour – darkness is my closest friend.

The psalmist calls on the God who saves him yet ends his prayer with the words 'darkness is my closest friend'.

I don't know about you, but that is not quite the uplifting encouragement I normally expect at the end of a psalm or a Sunday preach.

My key take-aways from this were:

1. Darkness can last a long time for a believer – we can be walking in faith and yet the outward circumstances of our lives don't change. The Bible does not give us false hope, but we can have wrong expectations that our faith protects us from bad stuff.
2. In darkness and adversity we learn about the grace of God. God is a God of grace, whatever we think about him at the time.
3. It reminded me of the book of Job – Job was angry but he still prayed and didn't turn away from God. We can hold on and pray to God regardless of our circumstances. The result was 'The LORD blessed the latter part of Job's life more than the former part' (Job 42:12). There is always hope.

The Bible doesn't sugarcoat the life of faith. It is full of stories about heroes of the faith who lived for a cause beyond themselves. Some of them overcame incredible odds in life and performed amazing deeds, some to die peacefully among their people, like David and Joseph, while others met gruesome ends, like pretty much all the apostles.

---

3 'How to Deal with Dark Times', www.youtube.com/watch?v=ulmaUtbayGY (accessed 30.11.23).

This is not pessimism. It is realism. But I was neither conditioned, educated nor equipped to face the dark journey.

The thing about culture is that it shapes what we believe and how we behave. Culture creates the norms by which we live and pervades the atmosphere around us. It shapes how we think and see what we see, and feel what we feel.

My journey with grief helped me understand that death and loss are taboo subjects in a Western culture that worships at the altar of success. We are conditioned to view death and loss as failures. That must change if we are to live life 'to the full' (John 10:10).

The price of judgement and silence

Silence is loud. It always has a price.

In 'Shine',[4] Joni Mitchell was coruscating about what she saw as the hypocrisy of a church that preaches one thing and behaves differently, in her lyric 'Shine on all the churches / that love less and less'. Closer to home, a friend of mine told me he lost his faith because the family's vicar said they were helpless to know how to support the family in their grief when his father died. The minister didn't know how to console them, didn't know how to help them grieve, didn't know how to empathise with them. It's that kind of experience that diminishes the relevance of the church to the reality and pain of everyday life.

To balance the books, it is also true that I have experienced and heard wonderful stories of love and compassion from all denominations of Christianity, truly excellent expressions of the love of Christ. But still it grieves me when I hear people angry with God because their fellow believers, including vicars, priests and pastors of different denominations, didn't know how to love them, comfort them, answer their awkward questions about how a loving God could allow tragedies to happen, about what happens now, even about what to say and what not to say, and when and how to say it. I know people who have left their churches because their grief has been ignored or downplayed. 'Jesus wept' (John 11:35) when he

---

4 'Shine' written by Joni Mitchell. Copyright © 2007 Crazy Crow Music. All rights administered by SONY/ATV Music Publishing. All rights reserved.

saw the grief of Mary and Martha – a church that professes the sacrificial love of Christ for all humankind weeps with the grieving and supports them through the journey.

We know a church can never be perfect because it is full of human beings like you and me, but the loving and open kind of response should be the rule and not the exception. A church that is called to be 'the light of the world' and 'a town … on a hill [that] cannot be hidden' (Matthew 5:14) should be the best in our communities and wider society at this stuff. It should be the rule for the bereaved to experience the love of Christ through the church and their fellow members. It should be the rule for the church that members know how to respond, to know the language for loss, to know how to behave when they see people overwhelmed by grief.

What about divorce and other grievous losses?

As Christians we diminish our capacity to touch the lives of people suffering loss when we fail to connect with the basic humanity of their experience.

As with bereavement, faith in Christ can seem irrelevant to the suffering and pain experienced in other kinds of grievous loss, such as divorce or loss of a career or a relationship, or loss of a future hope. It can be even worse when the response to loss seems judgemental.

Christians I know have gone through the pain of divorce, for example, and found their churches and friends silent or judgemental, leaving them feeling they have failed in their faith through their disobedience to the teaching of Scripture and the abandonment of their marriage vows. They feel judged and marginalised, as if they had taken their vows lightly and felt it was OK to break them at a whim.

None of the divorcees I know thought that way about the break-up of their marriages. One of my friends who had been divorced twice was the first person to recognise my grief when Vicky was still alive, when he said to me: 'You must be grieving at this, Roger. I know through my divorces the grief I felt to lose someone who is still alive.'

The depth of my friend's grief in divorce was a complete revelation to me and showed me how blinkered I had been to his reality, and how judgemental I had been in my unspoken attitude. I had been illiterate to his loss.

I had avoided even talking to him about his divorces and put them down as personal failures, taboo subjects to avoid. I realised I had just not been there for him or helped him in any way. I may as well have crossed the road. The reality he explained to me was far more complex than I had ever imagined.

His openness and willingness to talk prompted me to ask questions of other divorcees and the response of their churches, and sure enough their answers were similar. They not only felt grief but shame, marginalised and either rejected or ignored by their churches.

Jesus taught his disciples in the Sermon on the Mount: 'Do not judge, or you too will be judged … with the measure you use, it will be measured to you' (Matthew 7:1-2).

The price of our illiteracy in loss can give the impression of a hypocritical church that doesn't engage with the painful stuff of life and doesn't care, a church that says one thing but behaves differently. That's a heavy price to pay for lacking the language to encounter the reality and inevitability of loss as part of our human condition. The Christlike church acknowledges and deals lovingly with the reality of the losses that are so common in life regardless of how and why they happen.

If we struggle to connect with loss in the church, how can we connect with a world around us that is chock-full of such pain from loss? We have a massive opportunity to get to grips with the reality of loss in life among believers, so that the church can reassert its relevance to daily life in the communities it serves.

So, what can we do?

We can start by behaving differently. We can walk a different way if we talk and behave a different way.

To do that we have to start by understanding what loss is all about and what it does to the human spirit and soul.

Time to reflect

If you're anything like me, you need to think a bit about what you've just read before you move on to the next chapter. There really is no rush.

Why don't you take a few moments here to reflect on what you've read and ask yourself a few simple questions:

- How have you engaged with people who have suffered deep loss?
- How have you reacted to people going through divorce or finding themselves unemployed?
- How well prepared do you feel to get alongside people who are grieving?

Nobody is marking your homework, but you might also want to talk to a trusted friend or family member about your insights as you read the book.

It is not good to grieve alone. It's a journey and, like all journeys, it's better when it's a shared experience.

And just so that you are prepared, I'll be asking annoying questions at the end of future chapters as well.

Chapter Three: What is Loss?

Vicky died after a long and degenerative process that had reduced her to an infant-like state. Her death wasn't a shock when it came, and however painful and bewildering, it was also explainable medically and long expected.

All deaths are the same and all deaths are different. They are the same because they all signal the end of a living human being on this earth. Yet each death is different and individual in its own way. Many deaths are sudden, shocking, tragic and completely out of the blue. Some are sacrificial, dying for a cause or another person. Some seem completely meaningless and random. Some have an explanation. Others remain a mystery. Some are dreadful accidents, some are suicides, some are self-destructive, some are murders and some are executions in countries where capital punishment remains legal. Some confound every sense of humanity we possess. Some are plain unfair, inexplicable and unjust.

Your story will be different from mine, but I have little doubt that so much of our experience and learning will be common and applicable to us all.

No two deaths are the same. But they all cause grief and mourning.

Indescribable pain

La Vida es un sueño.
(Calderón de la Barca, 1636)

Don't bother with Google Translate – the quotation from the Spanish playwright Calderón means 'Life is a dream'.

It's late October 2020, and the world is going through the second spike of the COVID-19 pandemic. I'm driving to Southampton to celebrate the birthday of my five-year-old grandson, Joel.

I'm driving in the outside lane of the M27, listening to BBC Radio 4 *World at One*.[5] Same old subject headlining every day for more than six months – COVID-19. Only this time, as I listen, I start weeping uncontrollably and I can't stop.

My internal monologue kicks off: 'For goodness' sake, Roger, you're in the outside lane of the motorway, what are you doing? Don't be an idiot!' But I can't stop. I know the danger around me and the danger I now pose to other drivers. But I can't stop crying.

There's no hard shoulder on the motorway and no exit for several miles, so I must keep going. I'm in that crazy place where I know I am at risk and I'm a risk to others and there is nothing I can do about it other than steel myself and regain my composure as quickly as possible. I ease the car over to the inside lane and slowly get my brain back into gear. Safe again, at least for now.

Why?

The programme featured the story an Asian man aged seventy-eight who had caught COVID-19 and was admitted to hospital, desperately ill. His English wasn't great and so his thirty-eight-year-old son had somehow managed to persuade the hospital staff to allow him to stay with his dad and act as his interpreter, and he then became his main carer. The son said it had been a miracle he was allowed to stay because visitors, even close family, were banned under the COVID-19 restrictions on hospital and care home visiting.

As soon as the story started, I knew I should turn the radio off. It was too raw for me, the memories still too recent of Vicky's death in a care home that I was not allowed to visit. But I couldn't turn it off – I needed to know this story would turn out well. I needed hope. I needed to know that not every story would turn out like ours did. So, I listened. And I started to weep. And I continued to listen and to weep, regardless of the danger and traffic around me.

This wasn't some death wish on my part. It was the grief of my wife's death hitting me at the most unexpected moment when I needed to be in maximum control of my faculties. In the outside lane of a motorway with cars and lorries all around me. Thanks for that – perfect timing!

The story affected me so deeply, not just because it was another story

---

5 BBC Radio 4, *World at One*, 20 October 2020.

of lives torn apart by the dramatic effects of the pandemic, but because it reminded me of what I had been denied.

I had been unable to see Vicky during the seven weeks before she died. Her care home had 'locked down' and banned visitors, even spouses. Vicky had lost all her faculties for communication and no longer knew who I was, so I couldn't communicate with her by phone or Skype or FaceTime. Dementia truly is that cruel.

I couldn't be with her as she died. I wasn't allowed to see her body until twelve days after she died, until after the 'necessary hygienic preparations' had taken place. That was official speak to say she had been quarantined, followed by a special decontamination after a COVID-19 death.

The *World at One* story brought all this flooding back to me, uncensored and raw. And I was in the outside lane of a motorway.

Only I wasn't. I was in a highly dangerous dream-like space in-between the reality of driving my car and grief-filled memories that hurt like stink, with a pain beyond description in the English language. At no point was I thinking Vicky was at peace now, with the Jesus she so loved and longed to see. No spiritual platitudes or clichés in my head could lessen my pain. My mourning did not feel like I was being blessed in any way, shape or form.

That's what grief is like when it hits you like a wave out of nowhere. The rational bit of my brain said: 'Don't listen to this, it will feed your grief.' The emotional bit of my brain said, 'Carry on listening, you'll find hope, this story will end well.'

Thankfully I had the motivation to get to my daughter's house, to be with her and her family and the joy of my grandson's birthday celebration. And this hope 'in the moment' helped me regain control of both me and my car.

That's what grief does. Even though I know my life has meaning, and I know I am so fortunate to have a loving family and circle of friends, it sneaks up on you like an unexpected gust of wind that knocks you off balance, or a wave in the sea that you know is coming but still flattens you, winds you and has you gasping for breath.

When I think about my deepest moments of grief, they feel like some parallel universe where I am split in two – my rational self on the outside looking in and my emotional self deeply consumed by inexplicable, uncontainable and indescribable pain that I could not locate anywhere in my body but was deep in my soul.

My pain was caused by grievous loss.

I don't mean to sound morbid, but experiences like this taught me the inevitability of loss as part of this mysterious deal of being human. It comes with the territory, however much we love life.

Life brings loss

> Your loss is not a test, a lesson, something to handle, a gift or a blessing. Loss is simply what happens to you in life. Meaning is what *you* make happen.[6]

Think about it. Life brings lots of experience of loss. As David Kessler says, in the quote above, loss is simply what happens to us in life.

As a child I grew up in Liverpool, where my world was defined by the street where I played with my friends, and the short daily walk between home and my primary school. I was obsessed with football, occasionally got in trouble for breaking windows with a misdirected shot at the imaginary goal on the side wall of our house, learned to ride my bike in the street, and played in the sandhills of Formby beach most weekends in the summer with my mates, or football on the beach with my dad (he would have made a great sports coach in another life). I captained the school football team and I was in the school choir. I loved being outside and spent as much of my life as possible there. Those days there was less traffic and the streets felt much safer.

When I changed school at the age of eleven, I lost touch with teachers I loved and friends I would never see again. I went to a new school where they played rugby instead of football. I lost the joy of playing football every day in the playground with jumpers for goalposts and scuffed shoes, and on Saturday mornings playing for my school in games with proper goalposts, football boots and school colours.

I lost the convenience of living ten minutes' walk from school and suddenly had to leave home early every morning to catch a bus and travel forty-five minutes to a school on the other side of Liverpool. I lost the familiarity of seeing people from my neighbourhood every day on the way

---

6 David Kessler, *Finding Meaning* (London: Rider, 2019), p. 7.

to and from school and walking home with my mates. When I came home I had to do homework, and my friends couldn't come out to play football in the street anymore because they all had homework too.

And here's the thing. I didn't experience my change of schools as loss. Sure, I missed the security of my old school and the sense of familiarity and safety that came with attending a local primary school. I missed playing out in the street with my mates. I was excited *and* nervous, it was a new venture, a step into a big unknown, a big change in my life.

I had to wear a distinctive purple school blazer that gave me a new identity as part of a new tribe. The flipside was becoming a target for rival school tribes in a much bigger community, where nobody knew my big brother so they weren't scared of him, and he couldn't protect me anymore.

I had to learn and prove myself in a new set of subjects, with teachers who knew very little about me apart from my name – they didn't know my family or my life history, that I loved and was good at football, or had the voice of an energetic angel in the church choir (before it broke!). I had to learn new things and make new friends. I had to prove myself in a new set of sports that I soon learned to love.

Why am I making a meal of changing schools as an eleven-year-old? What's that got to do with loss? We all did it, didn't we, in the normal course of life? And that's my point.

However trivial this episode seems, in gaining something new I was losing something old. My juvenile self was growing into an adolescent who had to adapt and change in a wider and scarier world, newly separated from the familiar and safe everyday childhood world I had known. I just didn't see it as loss, I saw it as a natural thing, the stuff you do as you grow up. Just something that happens in life.

If you asked my mum, she would have experienced it as a loss. Instead of me coming home every day for lunch, I wasn't there at lunchtime. There was now a gap in her routine in the world. Her youngest son had to travel from one side of Liverpool to the other to go to school and wasn't a baby anymore. And isn't that the way with parenting? We want to see our children grow and yet it's painful when we have to let go of them so they can grow.

Change, in other words, brings loss as well as pleasure, adventure and gain. It's just that we don't count some losses as losses.

We do not see things as they are. We see things as we are.
(Rabbi Shemuel ben Nachmani, The Talmud)[7]

Many experiences of loss are far more painful than changing schools, and mark our lives deeply. They change how we see the world. Some losses change how we see ourselves so deeply that they change our identity and the course of our lives, especially when we feel we have had no choice or control in what has happened, and feel the loss as a great injustice.

Losing your job, your home, your marriage, a good friendship, a grandparent, a parent, a child, all change who we are and how the world describes us.

I will never forget registering Vicky's death, and the Registrar of Births and Deaths was taking my personal details. He asked my status and before I could say 'married' he said 'widower'. It felt as though he had stabbed me in the guts. It felt brutal. In my mind I was still married, and he had just changed my identity without my consent. Being told I was a widower felt genuinely violent.

In a similar story of insensitive official labelling of our losses, a close friend told me of the anger he felt after his divorce and being described by the Child Support Agency as an 'absent parent'. He dearly loved and continues to love his children from his first marriage. There was nothing remotely absent about him.

Some losses can violate you, strip you of your dignity, freedom or independence.

I remember returning to my car one day to find the window smashed and my bag of clothes stolen. I know it wasn't that big a deal compared to some of the more brutal violations many people experience, like physical assault, emotional abuse, bullying or even rape, and truth be told I didn't lose that much – but for days I felt personally violated, vulnerable and unsafe, as though it could all happen again, or something even worse.

Other losses leave us helpless and feeling disorientated. Our laptops and phones are stuffed with personal history, family photos and work files. Our wallets and purses contain our personal identity data and the basic ability

---

7 Anaïs Nin, *Seduction of the Minotaur* (Chicago, IL: The Swallow Press, 1973), p. 124. Nin attributes the original to Rabbi Shemuel ben Nachmani, as quoted in the Talmudic tractate Berakhot (55b).

to buy stuff or travel somewhere. Mislaying the keys to my house or car feels so much more than an inconvenience; it leaves me anxious about how I am going to manage life without them, and who has found (or stolen) them and what will happen next.

Loss can feel like you have been targeted and victimised. It feels like you have been stripped of something you held dear. You would never have chosen to lose it if you had only been given the choice.

Some losses make people feel angry with God. Why me? How could a loving God allow this to happen to me? Why didn't he answer my prayers?

These are the losses that fundamentally alter the course of our lives for better or for worse. They mark us for life. They are the ones we never forget – even though we may block them out from our conscious memories – because they are so deeply ingrained in our being, whether we care to acknowledge them or not.

Those kinds of losses really suck.

Those kinds of losses change who we are.

Love and loss

I hold it true, whate'er befall:
I feel it when I sorrow most:
'Tis better to have loved and lost
Than never to have loved at all.
   (Alfred Lord Tennyson, 'In Memoriam')[8]

There is no grading system for loss. I have lost count of the friends and family who have said they cannot imagine my loss. And my genuine response has been 'loss is loss is loss'. We cannot compare the emotional anguish of losing a middle-aged spouse to dementia, to that of losing a child from suicide at the age of nineteen or a parent to a stroke at the age of ninety-three.

And we can't begin to compare the death of someone we loved with the death of an abusive parent, spouse or sibling, where the emotions are so much more complex and can bring relief and grief in unequal measure.

---

8 www.goodreads.com/quotes/32569-i-hold-it-true-whate-er-befall-i-feel-it-when (accessed 30.11.23).

I experienced sadness at the death of my grandparents, but I can't say I grieved deeply. I knew I needed to be sad, but I was too young to understand the significance of their lives and who they were to me or to my parents and older siblings. They hadn't featured very much in my young life, so my attachment to them wasn't that strong. That meant my separation from them in their deaths wasn't very hard for me.

I really experienced grief at the death of a human being for the first time with the death of my mother-in-law from cancer in her early fifties and my father-in-law only a couple of years later. He died from heart disease, but I think it was really a broken heart. He had lost hope in his life after the death of his wife. I witnessed at first-hand Vicky's deep and inconsolable grief, and that of her siblings, at the loss of both their parents way too young.

I grieved at the loss of my brother-in-law from heart failure at the age of forty-seven. I saw how deeply his death affected Vicky, only three years younger than him. His death marked her life indelibly and deeper, I believe, than even her parents' deaths at their young age.

I grieved and mourned at the shocking death of my twenty-one-year-old nephew but couldn't ever come close to the experience of trauma and grief experienced by his parents and his siblings in their loss, which was made even harder to bear when the coroner delivered an open verdict, compounding their loss with no explanation as to the cause of his tragic death.

I grieved and mourned the death of my parents, my dad at the age of eighty-nine and my mum two years later at eighty-six. Their deaths were the first occasions I experienced waves of grief sweeping over me at the most unexpected times. Like in the shower in the morning and thinking I hadn't rung mum for a week or so, and then the penny dropped that the reason we hadn't spoken was that she was dead. Or after a good round of golf and I wanted to ring my dad and tell him about the amazing chip I holed for the only eagle of my life on the eighth green. And then realising I couldn't. He wasn't there any more to hear about the sporting exploits of his middle-aged son, who still wanted to share the childlike excitement of the moment with his dad.

But nothing, absolutely nothing, prepared me for the grief of losing my wife progressively over some ten years to dementia while she was still alive and breathing. And even those ten years of progressive loss could not prepare me remotely for her death.

I recall vividly one morning in the shower, as Vicky's condition deteriorated, weeping and crying out to God and asking why it all hurt so much. And I felt the Holy Spirit say to me, 'The measure of your pain is the measure of your love.' That's when I understood that love and pain are two sides of the same coin. The depth of my pain was the measure of my love for her. It opened my eyes to the pain of God at the death of his Son and the magnitude of his love for his children in that sacrifice.

It also helped me understand I was truly blessed to have experienced such love – it was a privilege to be treasured despite the pain and regret it brought.

> Grief is the price we pay for love.
> (HRH Queen Elizabeth II after the events of 9/11)[9]

Let me be clear that I am not talking here about the deliberate and abusive infliction of pain and loss to test another's love – this is not about manipulation and abusive relationships. That's a totally different situation about which I am not qualified to comment.

I repeat for emphasis. Pain and love are two sides of the same coin.

Kessler argues that: 'grief is optional in this lifetime. You don't have to experience grief, but you can only avoid it by avoiding love. Love and grief are inextricably entwined.'[10]

I don't know whether to agree with him about grief being optional because I have not avoided it. But I do know I haven't avoided love and I am grateful to have experienced it deeply.

I now understand everyone's grief is different and unique because every relationship is different and unique. There is simply no point comparing the loss of a parent, a child, a spouse, a sibling, a close relative, a friend or even a much-loved family pet because the pain of grief is proportionate to the strength of the attachment and love.

---

9 www.itv.com/news/2022-09-20/grief-is-the-price-we-pay-for-love-the-queens-final-journey-in-pictures (accessed 18.12.23).

10 Kessler, *Finding Meaning*, p. 9.

A bereavement is a painful separation from someone we have been deeply attached to emotionally, regardless of any genetic or blood ties, someone we have depended upon for whatever reason, someone who depended on us, and whose life has marked our lives indelibly.

That's why I think loss is loss is loss.

Time to reflect

It's time for a bit of reflection again. Why don't you take a few moments here to think about what you've read and ask yourself a few simple questions:

- What losses or bereavements have you experienced in life?
- How have you handled grievous losses in your life? Have you gritted your teeth and ploughed on or have you stopped to allow yourself to grieve?
- Has the loss of someone you loved made you afraid to love again?

Chapter Four: Wired to Avoid Loss and Pain

Our new Constitution is now established, everything seems to promise it will be durable: but in this world nothing is certain except death and taxes.
    (Benjamin Franklin, a Founding Father of the USA)[11]

I've never had a choice about paying taxes if I want to stay on the right side of the law. They are so embedded in daily life they are even hidden in the price of stuff I buy. To all intents and purposes, they are invisible, even though I know they are there. I am conditioned to pay taxes because they are simply part of our way of life, and pay for things like the National Health Service, education, highways and our government.

In contrast, I had little if any conditioning to handle the death of a loved one until it happened.

The big question is: why?

The weird thing is that we know that grievous losses have a deep impact on our mental and physical health, well-being and quality of life. Doesn't it strike you as perverse, therefore, that we are not conditioned for something that is 100 per cent certain to happen to all of us during our lives?

No one taught me a language for deep and grievous loss until I had truly experienced it. I had lost my parents and several close relatives over the course of thirty years, and I thought I had experienced grief. Losing my wife, however, was like being exiled into a totally foreign country whose unfamiliar customs and language I didn't even know existed, let alone understood, until I was immersed in it. And my stark choice was to sink or swim. This was different from anything I had ever experienced in my life. I was genuinely ill-prepared.

---

11 https://constitutioncenter.org/blog/benjamin-franklins-last-great-quote-and-the-constitution (accessed 7.12.23).

It wasn't just me. Family and friends close to me frequently felt helpless or ill-equipped to know how to provide the comfort and support I knew they wanted to provide.

I am not you

We are sculpted by the world we happen to drop into.[12]

I am not you. Sounds obvious, doesn't it?

We are different from each other and handle our losses and grief differently. I only know what I know and have experienced, as do you. Yet our collective experience and wisdom have the power to break the cultural taboo of death by normalising and treating it as a natural and inescapable consequence of life. We need to condition ourselves to handle loss if we are to live full and meaningful lives. I don't mean we should become blasé about death and loss. I mean we need to handle death with the humanity and dignity it deserves.

We will all die in due course. I don't know about you, but I'd rather my family and friends can accept it as the completion of my life, however it ends. It won't take away the pain of their grief, but it will make it easier if they know my wishes when it happens.

Vicky left us the gift of knowing, when she was well and of sound mind, many of the things she wanted both approaching and following her death. She was an exception to our culture. And I'm so glad she was. I am now trying to be that too. I invite you to join me.

Forgive me if I get a bit nerdy for a while, but something that really helped me through my grief was to understand a bit about my basic wiring as a human being. It helped me get to grips with how I was reacting and behaving through my various losses. It helped me understand I wasn't going mad.

Wired to avoid loss

Psalm 139:13 says:

---

12 David Eagleman, *The Brain: The Story of You* (London: Canongate Books, 2015), p. 9.

For you created my inmost being: you knit me together in my mother's womb. I praise you because I am fearfully and wonderfully made.

God didn't make a mistake when he designed our brains. As human beings he wired us to avoid loss and pain, to experience love, joy *and* fear. Neuroscientists say the bit of the brain called the amygdala – Professor Steve Peters calls it our 'inner chimp'[13] – exists to alert us either to threat or reward. Its most basic function is to ensure the preservation of the human species. The science of the brain is not a denial of the wonder of God's creation, it's a confirmation of it.

The amygdala is also the bit of my brain that triggers my flight, fight or freeze response under stress.

The Nobel Prize-winning economist Daniel Kahneman, in his work with Amos Tversky, captures this response in the concept of loss aversion. In *Thinking, Fast and Slow*, Kahneman writes:

For most people, the fear of losing $100 is more intense than the hope of gaining $150. We concluded from many such observations that 'losses loom larger than gains' and that people are loss averse.[14]

In a similar vein Ori and Rom Brafman write in *Sway* about the irresistible pull of irrational behaviour:

We experience the pain associated with a loss much more vividly than we do the joy of experiencing a gain.[15]

To quote the Brafman boys again:

The more meaningful a potential loss is, the more loss averse we become. In other words, the more there is on the line, the easier it is to get swept into an irrational decision.[16]

---

13 Professor Steve Peters, *The Chimp Paradox* (London: Edbury Publishing, 2012).

14 Daniel Kahneman, *Thinking, Fast and Slow* (London: Penguin Books, 2011).

15 Ori Brafman and Rom Brafman, *Sway* (New York: Doubleday, 2008).

16 Ibid., pp. 21-22.

But they are talking about the world of economics. What on earth has that got to do with the world of death and bereavement?

Wired to avoid talking about loss?

Like the Benjamin Franklin quote, in this world there are few certainties other than taxation and death.

Death is what Derek Prince calls 'the universal appointment'.[17] It's a solid bet. It will happen to us all. It's a dead cert. And losses tend not to come any bigger than the death of a loved one.

That's why I found it so important to understand about loss aversion – it was so I could learn how to deal better with the pain of loss, especially the kind that involves the ultimate separation caused by death and bereavement.

It just doesn't make sense to me now that we aren't conditioned to handle this stuff. We went to the moon and back in the 1960s, we now have robots replacing human beings in the world of work, in 2020 we learned to invent vaccines to deal with pandemics in less than a year (when historically it took ten to twelve years to develop and approve a vaccine), we can deliver things from A to B by drone for both beneficial and destructive purposes, Artificial Intelligence capabilities like ChatGPT could well have written this book, and deepfake technology has us questioning what is and isn't true. And yet… it just doesn't make sense that we leave people to experience bereavement and loss as and when it happens with no advance life training and preparation.

I don't think I was prepared spiritually for the death of my wife. I certainly wasn't prepared emotionally for her death. I had plenty of advance warning because I knew the diagnosis of dementia was a long death sentence. I discovered some helpful resources *after* she died. There is also a dedicated, gifted and qualified army of therapists and counsellors to help us cope with our losses. But all of that is *after the event.*

Don't get me wrong. I am not suggesting that post-event bereavement counselling and the emotional, psychological support provided by counsellors aren't necessary. They absolutely are. But our success and achievement-orientated culture means we are expected to 'get on with life' and 'move on,'

---

17 Derek Prince, *The End of Life's Journey* (London: Derek Prince Ministries, 2004).

that resorting to emotional and psychological support feels like a personal failure, a mental health issue and a problem to be dealt with rather than a natural, unavoidable and simply human episode in our experience of life.

It just doesn't make sense.

Yet it is exactly what the Brafmans are saying about the irresistible pull of irrational behaviour. The more meaningful the loss, the more averse we have become in our culture to talk about it. And the less we talk about it, the more harmful and sneakily toxic the loss becomes. That is not civilised in my book. We need to rethink what we mean by civilised.

I reflect that Vicky insisted we should make our wills when we were in our late thirties and I thought she was being a bit morbid. After all, we were indestructible at that age, weren't we? At least, I thought so then. But she insisted, not from fear, but because she wanted to be clear about who would look after our children if anything happened to us. She wanted to specify they must not be separated, and we openly discussed with the named family members our wishes to check they would honour a commitment to take on three young children and ensure they remained together.

Thankfully, that eventuality never came to pass. But it meant our wills were in place when she lost her mental capacity some twenty-five years later.

I really didn't want to countenance or discuss thoughts about death at that age. In retrospect, I realise I feared death and preferred to avoid thinking or talking about it. I didn't want to consider the possibility of me losing Vicky, or my dying and leaving our children without either or both of their parents. The absurdity is that I knew, deep inside, that one day I would die and that Vicky would too. How irrational is that?

The whole idea of dying was just too painful to consider, so I didn't consider it. Death was just one of those inconvenient truths that are too brutal to countenance.

Vicky, on the other hand, in full possession of her faculties, would talk about death and openly tell me and our daughters her wishes if she ever fell ill or became dependent. We all wanted to avoid the conversations, saying she was being morbid, she had a full life ahead and had so much to look forward to. But when she started to lose her mental capacity and ability to communicate her wishes clearly, we knew what the healthy Vicky would want for the incapacitated Vicky. And that meant our family decisions were easier, if no less painful, towards the end of her life.

I was too fearful to ask those fundamental questions, but she wasn't.

The glorious paradox is that our surviving loved ones pay the price by having to second guess our wishes if we don't have the conversations when we can. I don't want my children to have to have conversations with agonising decisions about me when I die when it is relatively easy to avoid if I tell them upfront while I am alive and kicking. And I guess you wouldn't want that for your loved ones either.

Paradox upon paradox – the apostle Paul was spot on the money when he wrote: 'For I do not do the good I want to do, but the evil I do not want to do – this I keep on doing' (Romans 7:19).

Why?

Maybe it's just too awkward to start such a difficult conversation, and we don't want to dampen everyone's optimism for life by seeming pessimistic? My question is why something that is 100 per cent certain to happen is viewed as pessimistic? I would be pessimistic if I took for granted that my death would be painful and drawn out. But to think I will die one day is not a denial of anything, it is simply realistic.

Pessimism is about fearing the worst. It isn't pessimistic to think about death.

Realism about experiencing loss and pain is biblical. In John 16:33, Jesus is speaking to his disciples and warns them of the persecution and pain they were about to experience at his death: 'I have told you these things, so that in me you may have peace. In this world you will have trouble. But take heart! I have overcome the world.'

It's realistic to think about death. It will happen to us all. So why not confront it? I reckon it's our inbuilt humanity, our aversion to loss that means we know these are necessary conversations, but we prevaricate and put them off until 'the time is right'. And the truth is that there is never a right time.

I now think the way Vicky spoke about death was her wisdom and a parting gift to us. Now I know she was the realist, and I was the one avoiding reality.

How do you have those conversations without upsetting everyone and spoiling the party?

I know my family will mourn my death, I know they will grieve, I know they will experience deep pain. I don't want that for them, but sadly it's not in my gift to control any part of that happening. But it is in my gift to remove some otherwise painful and avoidable decisions for them while I can by making my wishes clear while I'm still alive and bouncing. That way, too, there are fewer nasty shocks and potential for family divisions created by my will after my death. And I want them to know the measure of the pain they experience is the measure of their love for me and the gift of our love for one another.

Once we knew of Vicky's diagnosis and the likelihood she would die within the next few years, I decided to re-draft my will and consult all my children on what I was proposing.

I appreciate that what I am describing sounds rational, but it was also a highly emotional experience to have to face up to the practical stuff surrounding my death, and to make some of the choices I had to make.

I put in place a Lasting Power of Attorney (LPA) over my life in consultation with my family. They were things I needed to do anyway, if I didn't want to leave my affairs in a shambles after my death or possible loss of mental capacity, so I decided I should do all of that through opening up a conversation with my children. It was an emotional process for them as well, having to consider the thought that I would die when they were still grieving for the loss of their mother even while she was still alive. We didn't have to dwell on thinking how much longer I might live, but it meant we were able all to acknowledge the reality that one day I would die. I have also written a 'living will' that describes how I want my funeral conducted and what happens to my ashes. Yes, they will be my ashes, not a body gradually decomposing in a coffin. My choice.

I was delighted to learn that my children have now all made similar provisions for their own children and held the conversations among themselves about who will look after whose children in the event of tragedy. They don't want it, expect it or anticipate it. They enjoy their lives and delight in their families. They are not miserable pessimists. But they have faced the extreme possibility that it could happen.

Why me?

Grief helps us to recognise that while we are unique, there are aspects of human life in which we are neither exceptional nor special. Each of us will grieve uniquely but we will all be subject to grief in this life.

Anger is a common emotion in situations of loss. The circumstances of my loss felt unfair and against the natural order of things. A child should not die before a parent. A sibling should not take their own life. No one should die as an innocent victim of a random accident. No one should die a violent and cruel death as an innocent victim of a murderer. And in my case, no vibrant and healthy wife, mother and grandmother should contract dementia in the prime of life and die of COVID-19 in complete isolation from her family.

How we react emotionally depends on our perspective on what we see as the natural and 'fair' order of things. I confess I had gone through most of my life thinking stuff that affected and touched the lives of other people didn't apply to me. Thankfully I had never experienced unemployment, insolvency, divorce, homelessness, or hunger. They were the things that happened to other people. I had experienced episodes of ill health, exhaustion and anxiety, but never anything disabling or requiring radical treatment or long-term medication. And some would rightly say I had been very privileged in my life. I had somehow dodged the bullets that had wounded other people.

I admit, however, that I thought, 'Why Vicky?' when she was diagnosed. And of course, deep beneath that question were, 'Why *my* wife?' and ultimately, 'Why *me*?'

Three things helped me deal with the 'Why me?' question.

Firstly, it wasn't me – it was Vicky who was losing her mental capacity and the joy of her life.

Secondly, it was the family who were losing a greatly loved mother, grandmother and sibling, not just me.

And thirdly, and most crucially, I came to recognise and accept that I am not exceptional. I am not indestructible. I am just another human being who will one day cease to live on this planet.

So the question became: Why not me? What aspect of the human condition did I have that meant stuff like this shouldn't happen to me? Where was my birth contract that said that, unlike other people, I would never experience suffering or loss in this life? Why would insurance companies even exist, let alone flourish, unless sad, bad and unfortunate stuff always happens to people in the way it happened to me? How come my faith didn't protect me or give me a free pass from these disagreeable things?

Why *not* me? Switching the question saved me from the anger. It saved me from a deep sense of injustice. It didn't save me from the sadness, the loss, the pain and the grief. But it saved me from the bitterness that flows out of anger and a sense of injustice. I didn't have to think like a 'Why me?'

victim, where pain became toxic and corroded me inside until it expressed itself in ill health or, even worse, in addictions or violence.

How do we recognise the emotions we experience if we have never been taught the language?

Children aren't pre-programmed at birth to speak any specific language, and it's only when they are able to find the words to express what they are feeling and why they are feeling it, that they become able to manage their reactions.

David Eagleman writes in *The Brain*:

> Instead of arriving with everything wired up – let's call it 'hard-wired' – a human brain allows itself to be shaped by the details of life's experience.[18]

When did you last see an infant child born speaking fluent English? The reality is that we aren't born speaking any language at all. Eagleman again: 'We are sculpted by the world we happen to drop into.'[19]

A baby born in England to English-speaking parents is no more programmed to speak English than Japanese. The baby acquires their English language through the environment and language around them.

It's the same with adults when recognising and articulating their emotions has never been part of their development. I'm not arguing, by the way, for flaws in human development as excuses for violence and aggression – I'm arguing that our lives are healthier and more whole if we have language to articulate and understand why we react the way we react.

I also thought that it was my personal responsibility to do something about it. It wasn't someone else's responsibility. This wasn't something for the government or society to do. It was down to me. Just me.

Taking responsibility for my thoughts and emotions

In his powerful book *Staring at the Sun*, Irvin Yalom quotes the philosopher Schopenhauer:

---

18 Eagleman, *The Brain: The Story of You*, p. 6.

19 Ibid., p. 9.

Our greatest goal should be good health and intellectual wealth, which leads to an inexhaustible supply of ideas, independence, and a moral life. Inner equanimity stems from knowing it is not things that disturb us, but our interpretation of things.[20]

How we see what we see is at the root of our health and well-being – therein lies our 'inner equanimity'.

To quote Yalom again:

No positive change can occur in your life as long as you cling to the thought that the reason for your not living well lies outside yourself.[21]

Whatever our worldview, philosophy of life, faith or otherwise, if we live thinking that we have little or no control over our thoughts and emotions, the result is that we become powerless to affect the course of our lives. It's fundamentally the difference between the person who sees themselves as the victim of circumstances and the person who sees themselves as responsible for how they live their own life. It's the difference between the mindset of 'Why me?' and 'Why not me?' It's the difference between 'Why does nothing good ever happen to me?' and 'How can I turn what has happened to me into something that works for good?'

The reality of life is that rubbish stuff happens to us all. The experience of devastating loss is universal. Even if you cannot control the circumstances and the things that happen to you, you can control how you respond and think about them.

My reality was well described by Yalom when he wrote about a patient in his psychotherapy practice:

There are few ordeals more nightmarish than witnessing the gradual but relentless crumbling of the mind of a life partner [and the] final

---

20 Irvin Yallom, *Staring at the Sun: Overcoming the Dread of Death* (London: Piatkus Books, 2008), p. 113.

21 Ibid., p. 100.

horror for Alice when her husband of fifty-five years no longer recognised her.[22]

Vicky and I had been married thirty-six years when I first noticed she didn't know who I was. We were driving to a family wedding when out of the blue she asked me my name. It wasn't so much she asked me my name, but she followed up by asking me if I was Paul, her brother.

I was devastated. It was before her diagnosis of dementia, and we didn't know what was going on. It had happened to me with my mum in the last years of her life in her mid-eighties, but this was my wife in her fifties. It was one of those moments when the lights on the Christmas tree of her memory had started to flicker and fail. It was only for a few seconds, but it was another of those car-driving occasions when I had to battle to stay in control of the car. All sorts of thoughts were going through my mind as to the cause. And at that stage I was in denial mode about the possibility of dementia.

A few days later, when we were at home, I had to go out for some client work and went to her art room to say goodbye. I was wearing a coat and hat, and even though she was responding to me, she looked at me as though I was a stranger. I knew in my gut that she didn't know who I was. And it only occurred to me later that I could have been a complete stranger in her home and it would not have registered with her. All of which, with the gift of rational hindsight, was even more worrying for her safety, and I shouldn't have left her alone. But as with so many things that I now understand, my reason wasn't even in the room as I experienced the shock of seeing that my wife didn't know me. Yet when I returned home, she knew who I was again.

I know what it is to witness first-hand and over several years the 'gradual but relentless crumbling' of my life partner's mind. I would not wish it on anyone. But way before I had read any of Yalom's work or resources about bereavement, I knew I had to be responsible both for Vicky's and my own welfare.

Vicky had taken care of me when I had episodes of ill-health and emergency hospitalisation – it was time for me to take care of her. 'For better, for worse, for richer, for poorer, in sickness and in health'.[23] It was time for me to step up to the plate on the last clause of our marriage vows.

---

22 Yallom, *Staring at the Sun*, p. 38

23 www.churchofengland.org/life-events/your-church-wedding/planning-your-ceremony/ wedding-vows (accessed 30.11.23).

Lacking the language

How often have you felt completely inadequate to help someone's pain when they have lost a loved one? I know I have. I haven't known what to say or do, and yet I have had to say something.

It saddens me when I hear of people crossing the road to avoid speaking to a friend or neighbour who has been recently bereaved. It appears they don't care. Or maybe they are just in a hurry, and it isn't convenient to stop and talk. Or they might be thinking, 'Isn't it time they pulled themselves together and got on with life?', but don't want to appear crass and uncaring by saying so.

In most cases, I think it's because they don't know what to say, think or do. They don't know how to deal with the emotions that may come tumbling out. They are afraid of the 'snot and tears' or what might happen if they open up the subject, like picking at an emotional scar. They might be afraid of the embarrassment of someone crying on their shoulder in public – they are afraid of both causing and getting upset.

In fairness, it is a tough and sensitive gig. But when we have neither learned the language nor developed the emotional capacity to respond, it really is guesswork. It can be easier to avoid it altogether so we don't put our foot in our mouths. The unintended consequence is that it can leave the bereaved feeling like a social leper, someone to be avoided because of their emotional scars and weakness. And however irrational, they start to think that you're just a fair-weather friend who doesn't care. That's a big and painful price to pay.

All it really needs in those moments is a kind touch, a hug, an empathetic look, maybe a 'How are you today?', or a text saying, 'I'm here if you need a chat, but don't feel obliged to answer.'

Learning the language

Have you noticed how people generally avoid using the words 'died' and 'dead' when they refer to someone? I noticed that with Vicky. Doesn't that strike you as weird?

Our culture tends to soften the language, blur it, or use euphemisms to be kind. People use words and phrases like 'passed', 'passed away', 'found a place of rest', 'met their Maker', 'popped their clogs', 'shuffled off this mortal coil', 'gone to a better place', 'released from their pain', 'lost their life'. And so on. When what they mean is someone has died.

I'm not being critical of people using this kind of language, because it's what our culture has taught us to say. It cannot be a moral or emotional failure to lack the language for grief and death if you have never been taught it in the first place.

In the same way, we only learn the language for loss and grief by exposure to loss and grief. We acquire it by hearing and observing how others speak and deal with it. We develop the emotional capacity to respond to grief by seeing it in others at first-hand.

I saw it in my nine-year-old granddaughter when I was with her mum and her aunties dividing out Vicky's jewellery several months after her death. Vicky had had the wisdom to earmark many years earlier which of our daughters should have what items, and she had been meticulous in dividing out the precious items fairly between them. They had known for many years, for example, who would have her engagement ring, her wedding ring and her eternity ring. Vicky's gift to us again.

My granddaughter Annie watched in sorrow. She hadn't experienced a family death before. The whole process was very emotional for us all as adults. Annie was observing silently, but when she saw me overwhelmed and my tears flowing, she came and sat with me, holding my arm, not speaking but looking me in the eye, her eyes full of tears for my pain. She didn't have the words, but she had the emotional awareness to touch and comfort me, giving me her full attention.

And here's my point. Not knowing how to speak and feel about death and grief can't be a personal failure if you have never been exposed to influential people around you speaking about death and seeing their grief. You can't be accused of failing or being emotionally illiterate if no one ever taught you how to respond in the first place.

We are wired to avoid experiencing loss and pain. And in the same way we are *mostly* wired to avoid causing loss and pain.

So – if we are *mostly* wired to avoid causing pain (unless for something we believe to be a greater cause or good, or just from plain sadism!), I suggest we avoid talking about something that is 100 per cent certain to happen because we don't want to cause pain in the moment.

The other daft thing is that when we avoid talking about things we are genuinely thinking about – and who doesn't think about death? – then we are suppressing thoughts and emotions that will come back to bite us in later life, particularly in relation to our mental health and well-being.

Complex and contradictory things, aren't we?

We do what we don't want to do, and we don't do what we do want to do.

Time to reflect

Time for some more of those uncomfortable questions again. Please take a few minutes to reflect before you move on to the next chapter.

- How well has your family or cultural upbringing conditioned you to deal with loss?
- How strong is your sense of 'loss aversion'? Do you find yourself avoiding things you would really like to do because you fear loss?
- How well-equipped do you feel to have a conversation with someone about their loss?

Chapter Five: You Can't Judge a Book by its Cover

You can't judge an apple by looking at a tree.
You can't judge honey by looking at the bee.
You can't judge a daughter by looking at the mother.
You can't judge a book by looking at the cover.[24]

Bo Diddley's classic from 1962 now passes for homespun wisdom.

By the way, it was written by Willie Dixon, so he should really get the credit.

My grief brought a multitude of unwelcome and often conflicting emotions to the surface. I had to find language to deal with it to avoid getting stuck in a swamp of self-recrimination, shame, abandonment, betrayal and confusion. At times it was utterly overwhelming, and I ceased to function like a normal human being. But I was one of the lucky ones. At least I didn't have to deal with the well-meaning people I've heard so many stories about who would say insensitive things like, 'Haven't you got over your grief yet?' or 'Don't you think it's time to move on?'

The thing I found most helpful in my early wrestle with grief was to understand that I am unique. I don't mean this in a boastful or proud way; it is simply true. I have a unique fingerprint. The irises of my eyes are unique to me. My experience of life is unique to me. Your experience of life is unique to you. Nobody else in the history of humankind has been me except me. Nobody else in the history of humankind has been you except you.

---

24 'You Can't Judge a Book by the Cover' written by Willie Dixon. Copyright © 1962, 1990 Hoochie Coochie Music (BMI) administered by Bug Music Limited. Arc Music Corporation/ Jewel Music Limited. All rights reserved

I am the only person in human history to have experienced my losses in life in the way I have. No one else. Just me. And the same goes for you too. My experience of grief has been mine and mine alone. That doesn't make me special at all, because yours is yours alone too.

Do it your way

To be honest, I'm not a great fan of the Frank Sinatra 'I did it my way' philosophy of life that puts my ego and my way of doing things ahead of all other considerations. And in my more charitable moments I think maybe Frank didn't mean it that way, and I give him the benefit of the doubt. But on the topic of grief, there is only one way you can do it well, and that is your way.

David Kessler is an international expert on matters of grief and bereavement. He writes in *Finding Meaning*: 'Each person's grief is as unique as their fingerprint.'[25] Each of us in the family grieved Vicky's decline and death in different ways. I had regular episodes of uncontrollable weeping after her diagnosis. I couldn't have a conversation with anyone about her without breaking into tears. I tried. I even used to rehearse what I was going to say so that I wouldn't lose it in the moment and cause embarrassment for the person I was talking to. But I just couldn't hold back the tears. And if anyone showed me love and true empathy, that was a sure-fire way to get me weeping too.

I had to accept that this was who I am and this was how I was dealing with the loss. I gave these moments a name – they were my 'meltdowns'. Rather than thinking I was an emotional wreck and 'What's wrong with me?' I asked myself why they were happening, what was going on in me? The loss of my wife was the obvious answer to my deep sorrow, but that didn't explain why I cried when people were kind to me or kind to her. Those moments truly moved me, and I had to ask myself, why?

In exploring my reactions, I discovered the uncomfortable truth that I wasn't used to accepting people's love and kindness. I had tried to give love and kindness wherever I could – doubtless not always succeeding and frequently falling short – but my conditioning hadn't taught me to receive and accept love and kindness from people who expected nothing in return. I

---

25 Kessler, *Finding Meaning*, p.29.

could blame the 'niceness' of English culture or the legacy of Victorian values and Second World War stoicism to justify myself, or a lack of self-value and thinking I was undeserving. Or growing up in a culture where we are taught to look for hidden motives when we are given something, to think 'What's the catch?' because no one gives you something for nothing, do they?

It was my choice how to respond to people's genuine kindness, and I was the only one who could change the way I thought and stop thinking about offers of help and kindness in the way I did. And that's the thing about genuine kindness and unconditional love. They don't expect anything in return. They don't become a debt to repay. And if they do, then they weren't selfless and genuinely loving offers in the first place.

My meltdowns increased once it had become unsafe for Vicky to be at home and she had to be admitted to a dementia care home. I weep even now as I write, picturing the deep anguish in her face as my youngest daughter, Rachael, and I looked back at her as we left her in the first care home, and she had to be restrained physically by two care workers from running after us as we turned to wave goodbye with tears in our eyes. They became daily meltdowns after her death.

Each of our three daughters, all with families of their own, negotiated their loss in different ways, both after the diagnosis of dementia and after the death. The fact that they weren't reacting as I reacted, and they were each reacting differently from one another most definitely did not mean they were grieving any less.

In *Talking to Strangers*,[26] Malcolm Gladwell explores how misreading strangers can have disastrous consequences, with illustrations from history, psychology and infamous legal cases. He quotes the false conviction of Amanda Knox for the murder of Meredith Kercher in Italy in 2007. The evidence for the conviction relied heavily on reports of her behaviour after the discovery of her murdered friend, and it took eight years for the truth of her innocence to emerge and her release from prison. Gladwell writes:

> If you believe that the way a stranger looks and acts is a reliable clue to the way they feel ... then you are going to make mistakes. Amanda Knox was one of those mistakes.[27]

---

26 Malcolm Gladwell, *Talking to Strangers* (London: Penguin Random House, 2019).

27 Ibid., p. 171.

The way a person grieves and mourns a death is unique to them. We should not compare ourselves and think we are failing in some way if we aren't grieving as society expects. In my case, I certainly wasn't 'under-crying', and I found my meltdowns both cleansing and healing. Some might have thought I was an emotional wreck and falling apart. I wasn't. It was my way of dealing with the overwhelming sadness I was experiencing and was really part of looking after myself.

Kessler again: 'There's no right way to grieve – just different ways.'[28]

What about my faith?

I have experienced miraculous healings in my family, and I have heard multiple stories of healings from reliable and trustworthy people of complete integrity. The healing scriptures of Isaiah 53:5: 'and by his wounds we are healed' and of 1 Peter 2:24: 'by his wounds you have been healed' are foundational in the theology of my church and are regularly taught and prayed.

I know God can perform miracles that are beyond human understanding. I even wrote a book called *How on Earth Did That Happen?*, all about the power of God to perform miracles in my work and business career.[29]

Every day and every night, for years on end, I prayed for Vicky to be healed during my devotional time. I knew of friends praying and fasting for her healing. She read the healing scriptures over herself every day. But still her decline seemed inexorable as the dementia progressed.

Where was God in all of this?

Hearing from God

After the intensity of grief, several people have told me they thought they had stopped hearing from God in the pain of their circumstances. It's commonplace too for Christians to get angry with God and feel abandoned. They pray and don't hear any answers or have peace. They think God isn't hearing

---

28 Kessler, *Finding Meaning*, p. 32.

29 Roger Greene, *How on Earth Did That Happen? When Heaven and Work Collide* (Portsmouth: Great Big Life Publishing), 2017.

them or their prayers are inadequate. As a result, they stop praying, start to doubt their own faith or even start to doubt the existence of a loving God.

The thing about hearing from God is that it either prepares us for what's coming or gives us insight into what has happened. The prophetic[30] isn't divination or fortune-telling – it can be preparatory or explanatory. Sometimes it prepares us for blessing. Sometimes it explains blessing. Sometimes it prepares us for adversity. Sometimes it explains adversity. Sometimes it helps us make sense of our present reality. Sometimes we will need a word of biblical truth, sometimes a word of encouragement, sometimes a word of comfort, sometimes it will be a question we need to resolve, sometimes it will be an advance warning, and sometimes it will be the light-bulb moment when we understand why something happened. In my case, I experienced them all in the journey with Vicky. They weren't necessarily what I wanted to hear, but they certainly prepared me for what was ahead. And they all showed me that God was on my case and had not forgotten me in my pain.

As with any relationship, our relationship with God depends on the time we spend together. It's easier to hear someone when we can distinguish their voice from the rest of the noise in our heads and our internal monologues, in times of distress.

Being on God's frequency requires discipline and regular practice. Part of my discipline of spiritual self-care is to spend devotional time with God every morning. It is the first meaningful thing I do every day after making a cup of tea. I can't have a relationship with God or hope to hear from him unless I spend dedicated time with him. I reckon he is chilled about me doing that with a cup of tea in hand.

I find it easier to connect with God when I start with worship. I can't put a precise timeline on this, but there was a point in the journey with Vicky where I had to surround myself with worship, not to avoid the reality of what was happening but to reorientate what was happening in me and how I experienced that reality. I would start my devotional time listening to worship songs with my headphones on.

Over the course of something like five years, God gave me what I can only describe as a 'worship anthem' for each stage of the journey. The first of them was a track performed by Jesus Culture and Chris Quilala called

---

30 By prophetic we mean a supernatural enabling by the Spirit of God to hear his voice to foreshadow events that happen in the future. Some refer to it as a 'witness of the Spirit'.

'Your Love Never Fails'.[31] The words of the song echoed the promise of Psalm 30:5, 'weeping may stay for the night, but rejoicing comes in the morning' with the truth of Romans 8:28, 'we know that in all things God works for the good of those who love him'. The song clearly spoke into the reality of our circumstances and gave me the hope of joy returning in the metaphorical morning. It certainly didn't feel that way; the circumstances hurt like stink and my reality seemed a contradiction of what they were singing. I could see Vicky's capacity to deal with life declining gradually and irrevocably. Yet I knew the truth of God's promise expressed so clearly in Romans 8:28. That scripture became my anchor throughout the journey with Vicky. Whatever the journey threw at us, it was a truth I could hold on to, to give me hope and assurance that there was meaning in the painful maelstrom.

Something good had to come out of this. If not, either I was a naïve idiot or God's Word was a lie.

I now recognise this as the period when the Lord was starting to clothe me with the 'garment of praise' (Isaiah 61:3) to replace my despair.

Spiritual oppression

I went through two distinct cycles of grief with Vicky: the first after her diagnosis with dementia and the second following her death.

In the first cycle of grief, the four years between her diagnosis and death, I discovered there is an enormous difference between spiritual oppression and the normal human emotions experienced in grief. I think of spiritual oppression as being so overwhelmed by grief that it took me over and became part of my identity. It shaped my life, how I saw the world around me and related to other people. I saw myself as a grieving man, consumed with the pain of my loss even while Vicky was still alive.

The best way to explain the difference between this spiritual oppression and the healthy human response to loss is to describe what happened to me.

One Sunday morning a couple of months after Vicky's admission to the care home, I was at church. The teaching that morning was about worship

---

31 'Your Love Never Fails' written by Anthony Skinner and Chris McClarney. Copyright © 2008 Integrity's Alleluia! Music; Out Of The Cave Music; Thankyou Music. Administered by Integrity Music Ltd.

and how worship may not change the circumstances around us but it changes us and how we relate to the circumstances. During the time of worship, a young woman went up to the platform and began to sing spontaneously that God wanted to heal people in their worship. In her song she listed several medical conditions, but also sang about people being released from grief.

When she sang about being healed from grief, I had an immediate bad reaction. I thought, 'How dare you sing about my grief! My grief is my grief!' I was angry. And then the Holy Spirit spoke to me and said, 'That is exactly why you need to be released from your grief.' The worship continued and I knew I had to go forward and kneel before the platform to ask for God to release me from my grief.

There was no laying on of hands[32] in prayer by anyone ministering at the front, just a crowd of people worshipping the Lord, some standing, some sitting, some kneeling. As I knelt, I had a clear vision of Jesus weeping for me, just as he had for Mary, Martha and the Jews in those moments before he brought Lazarus back to life in John 11. A few moments later, one of the church leadership team came and placed his hands on my shoulders. I had not spoken to him or told anyone why I had joined the crowd at the front, but he just said to me he had seen 'a spirit of grief' lift from my shoulders. That was the point I knew I could grieve my loss of Vicky, but I did not have to be oppressed by a spirit of grief. I did not have to be a grieving man, but I was free to be a man who was grieving. Grief was no longer part of my identity, even though I was fully free to grieve.

The experience of release from an oppressive spirit of grief helped me enormously. I could allow myself to process the emotions of grief but still live and embrace life. It didn't mean my grief and emotions were any less raw, painful or powerful, but they no longer defined me.

In the intense period of grief following Vicky's death, my emotions were magnified to the extent that they often overwhelmed me. Ask anyone who knows me and they will tell you I'm a pretty rational bloke. Trying to reason my way out of my emotions, however, at the intense stage of grief was pointless. It just didn't work. I didn't try to suppress my emotions when they welled up. If I needed a meltdown, I would allow myself to have a

---

32 In the New Testament the laying on of hands is associated with Christ healing the sick (Luke 4:40) and after his ascension, the receiving of the Holy Spirit (see Acts 8:14-19). Initially the apostles laid hands on new believers as well as believers.

meltdown. I became so well-practised that I couldn't suppress my emotions even when I tried. I wasn't oppressed by a spirit of grief, but I was free to embrace my grief fully. I had learned the hard way that life had simply not prepared me to deal with grief of this nature.

Spiritual oppression may well be an attack of the devil. The emotions triggered by grief, however, are perfectly normal.

Prophecy

Sometimes we hear prophecy for ourselves and sometimes it is through others expressing what they have heard. We know it is for us because of the 'witness of the Spirit'.[33] Sometimes it is in a 'spiritual' setting, on other occasions it can be in the middle of a seemingly ordinary conversation when you get that 'gut feel' that brings a new insight or answers an outstanding question for you.

Whichever way, it is God communicating with us. My test of the prophetic is whether it materialises into something concrete or bears fruit: 'Make a tree good and its fruit will be good, or make a tree bad and its fruit will be bad, for a tree is recognised by its fruit' (Matthew 12:33).

My wife was full of faith and loved the Lord. Our church, including the leaders, prayed fervently and some even fasted for her healing over several years. Along with many others, I prayed the healing scriptures over Vicky for years on end:

He took up our pain and bore our suffering … and by his wounds we are healed.
(Isaiah 53:4-5)

'He himself bore our sins' in his body on the cross, so that we might die to sins and live for righteousness; 'by his wounds you have been healed.'
(1 Peter 2:24)

For I am the LORD, who heals you.
(Exodus 15:26)

---

33 In Romans 8:16 the apostle Paul says, 'The Spirit Himself bears witness with our spirit …' (NKJV).

But here's the freaky thing. I know the Lord speaks to me through the Holy Spirit. I have enough concrete evidence in my life to know that is true; I have seen his hand at work in impossible situations and in completely countercultural ways. They have all been times when I had a 'witness of the Spirit' that what I had heard or sensed was true, however unlikely the situation. I am happy to be counted a fool for Christ[34] in this aspect of my life.

I also know I have sometimes fooled myself into thinking I have heard the Holy Spirit speak to me when I had only been trying to convince myself of what I wanted to happen.

In praying for Vicky, however, I had never had the conviction in my spirit that she would be healed. Not once. I felt guilty. I felt my faith was failing. I felt I was letting her down.

Then one morning I was praying and the Holy Spirit asked me a question: 'Who told you my truth is only for this life?'

He followed the question with an assertion: 'My truth is eternal. Vicky may not be restored in this life, but she will be restored in my eternal life'.

I wondered if I had heard correctly or was just consoling myself again. Even if I had heard clearly, I didn't feel free to share it widely at the time because I thought people would question my faith. I now share it freely and know that it was true. God was preparing me for Vicky's death and reassuring me that he was hearing my prayers, even if I wasn't getting the answer I wanted.

After all these years my question now is: what makes us think the truth of Scripture is just for this life? What makes us think God has abandoned us if we don't get the miracle of healing in this life? Isaiah 40:8 says clearly: 'The grass withers and the flowers fall, but the word of our God endures for ever.' Call me pedantic but I understand *for ever* means *for ever*, for all future time, for always, for eternity. I stand to be corrected, but I am unaware of there being one Bible for this life and another one for the rest of eternity.

The reality for me changed with what I heard from the Holy Spirit that morning. It changed my mindset. My prayer changed from praying for Vicky's healing to lifting her before the Lord and asking that his will be done in her life. As simple as that. If he planned to restore her in this life, let it be done. If he planned to restore her in eternal life, let it be done.

We aren't meant to know it all: 'For now we see only a reflection as in a

---

34 1 Corinthians 4:10.

mirror; then we shall see face to face. Now I know in part; then I shall know fully, even as I am fully known' (1 Corinthians 13:12). I know God heals the sick. But I also know he doesn't always heal in the way we would like. My friend Alastair Mitchell-Baker has a gift of healing and has written a book called *We All Get to Play*.[35] He writes about the miracles he has seen, but also about his unanswered prayers for healing. They are the ones where he doesn't try to figure out why the prayer seemingly went unanswered. Instead, he pops them into his 'mystery box' and doesn't waste time agonising over whether he heard correctly from the Lord or his faith was weak. He just acknowledges that God's will is sometimes unfathomable for us and we hear imperfectly.

Premature death doesn't happen because our faith is too weak. It happens because we are humans living in an imperfect world. Things will happen in our lives where we can never work out why, we cannot figure out cause and effect. Now that I follow Alastair's advice and pop them in my mystery box, I spend less time and energy trying to work out the things that are beyond my understanding. I don't waste time stressing over what I can never undo or change. There is simply nothing to be gained from such introspection.

Our faith works when it is aligned with God's will for our lives. And God's will is for us to glorify him in this life and spend eternal life with him in the next. It's when we understand life on earth as the temporary bit in the context of eternity that we get the proper perspective.

God in and on my case

There were other clear moments for me in the journey with Vicky where God showed me he was both in and on my case. They were not at all enjoyable, but they were preparatory moments when I knew Jesus was weeping with me. I will share some more instances, not for purposes of self-indulgence, but to show the reality of his presence in our painful journey.

Some two years before Vicky died, a friend who had spent time looking after her in our home wrote me a long letter describing the vision God had given her. She had been reluctant to share it with me and, before doing so, checked with her husband, who cried when he read it but agreed she should send it.

---

35 Alastair Mitchell-Baker, *We All Get to Play* (Portsmouth: Great Big Life Publishing, 2019).

The vision described the journey ahead in metaphor, seeing Vicky as a rose named La Reine Victoria that had flowered beautifully in a warm garden before being overshadowed by a large tree outside the garden. The tree deprived her of light and nutrition, to the point the plant was dying. She had to be uprooted and tended in a large greenhouse until the day I would visit the greenhouse and find her gone, leaving only a rosehip in her place for the gardener to hold and tend.

I didn't share the vision with anyone, not even with our daughters. It contained references my friend could not have known about and resonated so clearly with what the Lord had shown me that I knew it to be true. But it was too painful. The large tree outside the garden was her dementia. The greenhouse was the future care home in which she died. The gardener was Father God.

The day after Vicky died, some friends who knew nothing of this prophetic vision left flowers on my doorstep. They were roses. Not only were they roses but La Reine Victoria roses. The prophetic vision had prepared me. God was now showing me it was his will to take her.

Sometimes the Holy Spirit asked me questions rather than giving me answers. A vivid example was the difficulty we had finding a suitable care home for what I knew were going to be the last years of Vicky's life.

About four months before she needed admission to a care home, I had started to look for suitable places. I only found one that I regarded as a potential long-term home for her, but it was full and had a long waiting list. Months later, when it had become unsafe for her to be at home, and with the help of Social Services, she was accepted into two consecutive homes where she was like a caged bird trying to escape, and they were clearly unsuitable environments for her long-term care. She was refused admission to another care home because of her behaviour and labelled an escape risk. I had contacted the original care home of my choice and their waiting list was no better than before. I had contacted multiple care homes who were all in the same situation of waiting lists or lack of suitable accommodation for someone with Vicky's needs.

I was both desperate to find somewhere suitable and frustrated at the inadequate state of care home provision for people with dementia, especially middle-aged people.

We were eventually offered a place that would be available in a couple of weeks' time following refurbishment. It was expensive, the environment was not ideal, but it was a clear improvement on where she was. I accepted provisionally and they agreed to keep the room open for her, but I would have to commit definitely within a week.

I was unsettled. I felt the home was OK and a big improvement, but not God's best for her. Then one morning the Holy Spirit asked me a question: 'If a care home was to ring you tomorrow to offer a room, which would you want it to be?'

My immediate response was St Rita's, the care home I had visited first, run by a charitable order of Catholic nuns. But that seemed pretty hopeless as I had checked with them again recently and there were still no places.

Tomorrow came and went, and I thought I had just been deluding myself again.

The following day, however, I found a voice message on my answerphone from the manager of St Rita's asking if I was still interested in a place as one had just become vacant. He agreed to assess her and the rest is history.

To cut a long story short, that was where she lived for the next eight months of her life, in a comfortable and modern home deep in beautiful countryside surrounded by the animals and wildlife she so loved, where she could roam in secure but spacious gardens, walk up and down the long corridors of the home to her heart's content, make new friends and eat well. God had come through for us again.

You already know that Vicky subsequently died in the care home in the first wave of the deadly pandemic. The care home had taken every possible precaution against what was an unknown threat at that time. They had closed to visitors well ahead of any national restrictions or lockdown.

On 14 April 2020 in the morning the doctor covering the care home rang me. She told me it was a routine call and there was nothing to be concerned about. She just wanted to have a conversation about my wishes if Vicky caught COVID-19 and required hospitalisation. She knew we had an Advance Order in place that Vicky should not be resuscitated – but this was a different scenario where she might well be fully conscious but need oxygen support for her breathing, or even to be placed on a ventilator if she could not breathe for herself. As a family we had previously discussed the possibility of her needing intensive care in hospital and had agreed we did not want her to experience the stress and distress of going into such an intimidating environment where she could not express herself or have any capacity to understand what was happening to her. The conversation with the GP was painful, but we were able to agree that her best interests would be served by remaining in the care home if she contracted COVID-19.

Just two days later, on 16 April, the care home manager rang to request my consent to test Vicky for COVID-19. She was showing signs of a high temperature and cough, together with a mysterious rash on her back. The call from the GP had prepared me, however painfully, to the reality that Vicky might contract this deadly virus. And now she had.

To make things worse, I was unable to visit her to see how she was, and I had to rely on daily phone calls to the home. By the end of her first week with the infection, the care staff told me she was stable and seemed to be improving. Though unable to explain to anyone how she was feeling, she was eating and drinking almost normally.

On the morning of 24 April, in my devotional time with God, the Lord showed me a clear vision. Vicky had told me regularly during her life of a dream she had as a five-year-old. In her dream she saw Jesus playing with a group of children in a garden. She ran towards them, wanting to join in. Jesus held up the palm of his hand and told her: 'Not yet. It is not your time.'

That morning, two days before she died, the Lord reminded me of her dream. Only now, Jesus was seated in the garden and beckoning her to come and join him. I knew it was her time. Despite the reports of her improvement, I knew in my heart that the apparent improvement was really that last burst of life and energy that seems so often to precede death. Once again, the Lord had prepared me for what was to come.

However painful the journey, however grievous my loss, however overwhelming my grief, these were all clear signs to me that the Lord was both hearing and watching over me.

Engaging with the reality of death and grief

I have attended multiple funerals in a variety of Christian denominations, all with consoling sermons and messages about the departed person and their eternal destiny, free from pain and suffering. I hold my hand up for having uttered countless platitudes to grieving families in the attempt to console them in their grief and pain at losing babies, children, spouses, partners, brothers, sisters, mothers, fathers, grandmothers, grandfathers, aunties, uncles and friends.

Here's the odd thing. I haven't been a practising Christian all my life, but let's say I have been for around forty years. Let's assume I've attended church in one form or another at least fifty times a year, not counting midweek meetings. Let's say I have heard upwards of 2,000 sermons and counting. Let's agree on 2,500. I have also read a few books along the way and listened to some great teaching in a variety of media, from tapes to digital downloads. I haven't agreed with them all, several have made me feel uncomfortable, some have been plain misleading, and I have seen fads and fashions come and go like any other walk of life. But they have mostly all contributed to my spiritual formation, including the things I disagree with as well as what I accept and believe. And let's face it, they have informed my biases too.

Among those 2,500 sermons, I've heard plenty of core gospel messages about the resurrected Christ overcoming death and hell after his crucifixion on the cross. I have received lots of teaching about divine healing, and I have participated fully in fervent prayer for healing to overcome life-limiting diseases or conditions, including Vicky's.

My only memory of those 2,500 sermons teaching me how to prepare for the emotional reality of death or grievous loss in bereavement was in my mid-thirties when I was attending a church service, standing at the back cradling Rachael, our six-month-old baby, as she was crying and unsettled. I'm guessing the sermon was about forgiveness and resolving differences with our loved ones – but I don't really remember a thing the preacher said. My guess about the subject matter is because I only remember him playing what turned out to be one of the most influential songs I've heard in my life. It wasn't a 'Christian' song. It was 'The Living Years' by Mike and the Mechanics:

I wasn't there that morning
When my father passed away
I didn't get to tell him
All the things I had to say
I think I caught his spirit

Later that same year
I'm sure I heard his echo
In my baby's newborn tears
I just wish I could have told him in the living years.[36]

Tears filled my eyes as I looked at Rachael. Cradling her made it especially poignant. I decided that I never wanted my children to have any unresolved issues with me at the end of my life – to the extent that I could help it.

I also decided I never wanted to have any bitterness or anger in me caused by unresolved issues with my parents, siblings or wider family while we were still all alive and able to resolve them. And I'm thankful that resolution in my mid-thirties helped me to navigate the close family losses of life without any sentiment of bitterness or regret. It also meant a lot of introspection as to my own part in those differences, and forgiveness where I knew the differences were unintentional. And while I cannot completely control it, I truly hope those I leave behind will not carry any unresolved issues with me.

I'm so glad I was there that Sunday morning. That song shaped my resolution to deal with family matters in the living years from that moment forward.

Apart from my Mike and the Mechanics moment, however, I cannot remember a single sermon telling me that the death of a loved one is incredibly painful and can make you feel you have lost the plot and are out of control, quite apart from the challenge it may present to your faith. Nor can I remember a sermon advising me how to help anyone else going through the deep valley of grief that is caused by traumatic loss.

Is it that we just don't know how to reconcile the pain of grief with a gospel of hope and love? Do we sweep it under the carpet because we want to promote a gospel of hope without paying a price in suffering? Does the idea of facing death make us too uncomfortable? Are we teaching transactional Christianity where faith in Christ means the pain of life melts away, and where our prayers are answered like some divine ATM dispensing blessings instead of cash?

Or have we passively adopted the practice of spiritual bypassing?

---

36 'The Living Years' written by Michael Rutherford and B.A. Robertson. Copyright © 1984, 1988 Michael Rutherford Publishing Ltd, and R&BA Music Ltd. All rights reserved.

Spiritual bypassing

Dr Craig Cashwell is a professor in the Department of School Psychology and Counsellor Education at the University of North Carolina, and he talks about the notion of spiritual bypass when Christians cannot handle the sadness of someone who is grieving and can only respond with spiritual platitudes, or spiritual ideas and practices as a crutch to cope with pain or trauma. Maybe it's that moment when we avoid something difficult by offering to pray or quoting Scripture because we cannot engage with or truly empathise with the sufferer's pain. Other examples of spiritual bypass are things like toxic positivity, compulsive goodness and forced forgiveness. He writes about validation of what someone is experiencing through normalisation as a key part of the healing process, integrating psychological wholeness and wellness with the spiritual.[37]

Spiritual bypassing (or whitewashing) can apply in all spiritual traditions and is also described as the act of using spiritual beliefs to avoid facing or healing one's painful feelings, unresolved wounds, and unmet needs. It is a state of avoidance where our spirituality justifies living in a state of inauthenticity. It helps us avoid the unwanted aspects of our own feelings in favour of what is considered a more enlightened state.

Now I know spiritual bypassing to be 'a thing' I can name it when I see or hear it, especially when I hear it from my own mouth. It helps me process how I am interacting with the person in front of me. It helps me know when I'm in danger of falling into the pit of empty platitudes. It gives me a fighting chance of helping the person in front of me to feel heard.

Grief is biblical

How do we deal with grief in the church?

In much of my biblical education, I was taught (correctly) to 'put off your [my] old self, which is being corrupted by its deceitful desires, to be made new in the attitude of your [my] minds; and to put on the new self, created to be like God in true righteousness and holiness' (Ephesians 4:22-24).

---

37 Craig Cashwell, Pennie Johnson and Patrick Carnes, *Shadows of the Cross: A Christian Companion to Facing the Shadow* (Carefree, AZ: Gentle Path Press, 2015).

I was taught that among other obvious sins, emotions like anger, jealousy and envy are 'acts of the flesh' (Galatians 5:19-21). Christians are not meant to act on these emotions or create discord. I was taught they were my 'self-life' or my 'flesh life' to be ignored. Yet they were precisely examples of my human emotions in grief, and most particularly in the intense period of grieving.

As believers we are rightly taught to resist temptation and take every thought captive.

> Submit yourselves, then, to God. Resist the devil, and he will flee from you.
> (James 4:7)

> We demolish arguments and every pretension that sets itself up against the knowledge of God, and we take captive every thought to make it obedient to Christ.
> (2 Corinthians 10:5)

Elsewhere the Bible teaches us that the 'testing of [our] faith produces perseverance' (James 1:2-3). And those who persevere under trial 'will receive the crown of life' (James 1:12).

Psalm 23 tells us:

> Even though I walk through the valley of the shadow of death, I will fear no evil, for you are with me; your rod and your staff, they comfort me.
> (v. 4, NIV 1984)

Even though I walk through the valley of the shadow of death, not *if* …

All these scriptures tell us clearly that faith does not mean some trouble-free walk in the park but it is a guiding star to help us navigate the troubles and losses of life, with the Bible as our handbook.

In summary, my Christian discipleship journey taught me my spiritual response is to lean on God in times of trouble and ignore (more accurately, bury alive) many of the things that make me human – my emotions, my thoughts, my will, my reason, my gut, the excruciating pain in my soul. It felt like a binary choice between my spirit and my soul, like they were separate parts of me that could be partitioned off. If I turned on my spiritual lights, I could then turn off and ignore what was going on in my 'self' or 'flesh' life.

It was only by going through my 'dark night of the soul'[38] that I delved deeper into the biblical truth about grief.

Look at King David – the man after God's own heart.[39] In chapters 18–19 of 2 Samuel, we see how David grieved deeply the death of his son Absolom at the hands of his army – a completely irrational response when we see Absolom had conspired to overthrow him as king and kill him:

> And for the whole army the victory that day was turned into mourning, because on that day the troops heard it said, 'The king is grieving for his son.'
>
> (2 Samuel 19:2)

Isaiah the prophet foretold the coming of Christ as 'a man of sorrows, and acquainted with grief' (Isaiah 53:3, KJV).

In the shortest verse of the whole Bible, it says, 'Jesus wept' (John 11:25). The scene is where Jesus arrives at the tomb of Lazarus and sees Mary, Martha and the Jews accompanying them weeping for Lazarus. We all know what happened next, but please check the preamble. It took Jesus two days after finding out Lazarus was sick and four days in all to get there. He didn't rush and he clearly knew what the outcome was going to be. He knew Lazarus would be raised from the dead for the Father's glory. And yet he wept. Was he weeping for his friend Lazarus? I don't know, but I suspect not because he knew the end from the beginning. I believe he was weeping out of compassion for those who thought Lazarus had died and they were mourning their deep and grievous loss.

I now understood that if it was OK for the Son of God, the man of sorrows, fully 'acquainted with grief', to weep even when he knew the glorious and miraculous outcome of Lazarus' resurrection, it was OK for me to weep as well, even when I trusted in his truth and the long-term outcome.

---

38 St John of the Cross, 'The Dark Night of the Soul', www.poetryfoundation.org/poems/157984/the-dark-night-of-the-soul (18.12.23).

39 See 1 Samuel 13:14.

I searched the Bible and found nothing telling me that when I gave my life to Christ I only gave him my spiritual life but kept the other parts of me back. The simple choice between my faith and my emotions is a false choice. When I gave my life to Christ it was the 'whole me', not only the spiritual me but the emotional, rational, hormonal, physical me – the whole nine yards, the whole shebang.

The combination of our reserved culture, my social conditioning and my incomplete understanding of the Bible had conspired to make me ignore and bury my emotions, to feel as though I was failing in many aspects of my faith if I allowed myself to feel emotions like anxiety, guilt, envy or fear. All of which is the worst possible route to follow for our mental health and well-being.

I now know that, especially in the intense period of grieving after bereavement, my emotions were often overwhelming and the way to overcome them was to allow them to surface and to process them. I had to name and understand them before I could take them captive; otherwise, I wouldn't know what I was taking captive. It sounds counterintuitive, but the only way to get past feeling down was to allow myself to feel down and work through it, not deny it, and only then could I 'make it obedient to Christ' (2 Corinthians 10:5). Not to stay there, but to work through it emotionally and spiritually. And my faith is not diminished by these feelings. It is reinforced by knowing that the emotions associated with grieving were fully embodied in Christ.

I don't let them own me or define me, but I don't bury them either.

As Churchill said: 'If you're going through hell, keep going…'[40]

Sin is in acting on the emotion, not the feeling of it. The apostle Paul wrote to the church in Rome: 'No temptation has overtaken you except what is common to mankind' (1 Corinthians 10:13). Experiencing what is common to humankind is not failing, it isn't grounds for deep guilt and shame. It is normal.

The circumstances of our losses may be infinite, and they may trigger genuine emotions ranging from shock through disbelief, denial, envy, anger, guilt or helplessness. Maybe even relief at the loss of an abusive family member, and then guilt for feeling relieved. It is normal. We don't need to beat ourselves up and consider ourselves as failing.

---

40 www.brainyquote.com/quotes/winston_churchill_103788 (accessed 1.12.23).

The reality is that death comes to us all some time or other in one way or another.

I tip my hat to the incredibly courageous sermon by Bill Johnson only three days after his wife's death[41] in 2022. Bill spoke of how life is full of loss and it's futile to try to figure it all out. The attitude we need is to be childlike, accept the mystery and trust him. My brain probably 'weighs about three pounds and has a volume of about 1,300 cubic centimeters',[42] but it cannot contain the ocean. I cannot explain this vast created world, yet I know it is real. In the same way, I could never adequately comprehend or explain its Creator, yet 'I know that my redeemer lives' (Job 19:25).

So what?

There are some excellent resources available in the UK through Loss and HOPE,[43] a coalition of organisations enabled by the charity AtaLoss,[44] and Care for the Family,[45] all of whom feel passionately about churches of all denominations across the UK being equipped in bereavement support. AtaLoss provide the Bereavement Journey course I experienced personally and Loss and HOPE are promoting the Bereavement Friendly Church charter comprising the twelve marks of a Bereavement Friendly Church. These materials and support are accessible to grieving people of any faith or no faith without preaching or judging. They love and embrace the bereaved regardless of their faith. That's my kind of Christianity.

But here's the rub. These were great resources to find *after* my loss. There was nothing in my experience of Christianity to prepare me *before* my loss, to know the emotional and practical turmoil I would face, to teach me the language of loss and how to respond in a healthy and life-giving way.

---

41 www.youtube.com/watch?v=USfftDqIx0Q (accessed 1.12.23).

42 https://askananthropologist.asu.edu/stories/brains-over-brawn#:~:text=The%20human%20 brain%20weighs%20about,the%20size%20of%20the%20body (accessed 1.12.23).

43 www.lossandhope.org (accessed 1.12.23).

44 www.ataloss.org (accessed 1.12.23).

45 www.careforthefamily.org.uk (accessed 1.12.23).

To speak of such things is far from a failure of faith – it is a genuine acceptance of our simple humanity.

We need a revolution in our thinking. We need to break some taboos. We need to front up to the inevitable reality of death and grief. Not just after the event, but before the event too.

We need to develop our language for loss. And just like our personalities and preferences differ, and just like our regional dialects and accents differ, it will be unique and different for each of us in how we give and receive love, support and comfort in loss and grief.

That's what Vicky did. And it was one of her many gifts to me and our children.

What does that language look and sound like? Through the book you will get a sense of how mine has developed. You will need to develop your own language for loss through reading and reflecting on the journey of this story through loss and pain, if you want to find hope and meaning beyond loss.

When we encounter people who are grieving, we need to stop assuming we know what might be going on in them when we look at the cover of their book. I wept a lot and had regular meltdowns. They weren't breakdowns (even if they might have looked that way to an outsider) but helpful emotional responses for me whenever I couldn't contain my sorrow. I wore my heart on my sleeve. If someone asked me a question, I would tell them the real answer. It was up to them, the listener, to decide how to react. Their reaction was not my responsibility – it was theirs and theirs alone.

That doesn't set any benchmarks for anyone else. In this respect Sinatra was right – I just did it my way. You need to do it your way. Just make sure you don't avoid it. Just make sure you do it.

Time to reflect

Please take a few moments again to reflect on this chapter. Here we go with some more questions to kick off your reflections:

- Do you feel as though you are expected to grieve in a certain way?

- What has the experience of loss meant for your faith?
- What does your worldview teach you about grieving?
- What assumptions do you make about someone's grief when you look at the cover of their book?

Chapter Six: Busting Myths

Loss takes multiple forms, but some losses go much deeper than others and penetrate to our identity, the very essence of who we are.

The death of a loved one is one such loss, and however short or long our lives, it is inevitable that one day we will die.

Normalising loss

The circumstances of a death may be horrendous and too shocking to contemplate: murders, executions, traumatic accidents, accidental killings. Too heart-breaking to consider: the stillbirth, the infant death, the teenager with their hopes and aspirations for life who dies from a drug overdose, the young mother succumbing to cancer, the loss of a child to suicide, the unexplained death with an open verdict from the coroner that leaves loved ones forever uncertain about the cause of death. People 'taken too soon'.

Alternatively, the death might feel like water torture, a slow burn with a terminal condition like incurable cancer, heart, lung or liver disease, or a progressive condition like dementia that chips slowly away at life so the person who dies is not the same person who lived and we loved so many years before. Or it might simply be slipping peacefully away in old age, a life well lived.

Where the death involves someone who was abusive, controlling or violent, it can feel like a blessed relief and a new sense of freedom for the bereaved.

The circumstances of death are infinitely individual, but the human experience of grief at the death of a loved one, triggering complex and often contradictory emotions, is pretty much universal in all but extreme exceptions. And that's the stuff we can learn to understand if we will only allow ourselves to acknowledge death as an essential aspect of life. We need to normalise the process and experience of grief in the teaching of the church if we are to help people in pain. We need to normalise loss and remove the taboos around grief. Like Jesus, we can weep with those who weep. It isn't failure or a lack of faith. The processes and emotions around the experience of grief are just plain normal and part of the deal of being human. We need to stop the spiritual bypassing and platitudes where Christians cannot handle the sadness of someone who is grieving. We need to respond with personal authenticity infused with genuine compassion. As Jesus did.

Spotting the dragons

I'm naïve and optimistic enough to hope some of you have read my first book *How on Earth Did That Happen?* If you did, you might remember me writing about my belief system building up in my childhood, teens and early twenties to the point where my adult spiritual life was surrounded by imaginary mythical dragons hemming me in and keeping me in my orthodox thinking box.

It wasn't until I had experienced the hard knocks of life in my working career and the wisdom and relevance of the Bible in dealing with those hard knocks that I came to see the dragons for the falsehoods and illusions they were. I had been conditioned to think in a particular way and found out the hard way that significant parts of my conditioning, the way I saw things, were just plain wrong. In the jargon of behavioural scientists, they were my self-limiting beliefs.

I suspect I'm not the only one to have a few dragons to slay in my self-limiting beliefs about death and loss.

How do we slay them? We start by naming, normalising, and subjecting them to the 'sword of the Spirit, which is the word of God' (Ephesians 6:17).

The problem is that we can thrash around wildly with our spiritual swords and simply wear ourselves out unless we know the enemy we are fighting. And maybe the devil and his demons don't have to try very hard, because our enemy is the way we have been conditioned to think. Our self-limiting beliefs often do their work for them.

I'll start by naming some of mine and get to work on slaying them. They may not be yours, or yours may be different, but I bet a few of yours and mine will overlap.

Dragon 1: Bad things don't happen to good people

By now I hope you are persuaded that loss and pain are a normal part of life, and that bad things happen even to good people. Does that mean the 'good news' of the Gospels, the book of Revelation's vision of heaven on earth, and the Bible's teaching about eternal life are all a big con-trick by the powerbrokers of the church to keep us in line in this life and ensure the church coffers are filled?

In a word, no.

If you need persuading that the Bible doesn't do spin, how about looking at the life of Job and his unwavering faith in God in the Old Testament despite the devastation of his family, his health and his wealth? The Bible tells us that he lost his livestock, his servants, his sons and daughters in four separate incidents all in one day.[46] You won't spot many gilded lilies in that part of the story.

The New Testament too is full of warnings about loss, suffering and persecution for the sake of the gospel.

How about zooming in on the story of Stephen in Acts 6, the man chosen by the apostles to oversee the daily distribution of food to the widows among the Grecian and Hebraic Jews? He was described as 'a man full of God's grace and power [who] performed great wonders and signs among the people' (Acts 6:8), only to be dragged out of the city and stoned to death by members of the Synagogue of the Freedmen, Jews of Cyrene, Alexandria, Cilicia and Asia.[47]

How about the reality of the life of the apostle Paul and his three epic journeys to spread the gospel throughout Asia, constantly being expelled from their cities? To name just two incidents, he and Silas were stripped, beaten, 'severely flogged' and thrown into jail in Philippi (Acts 16:16-24). In Lystra he was stoned to within an inch of his life and left for dead by Jews from Antioch and Iconium.[48]

The teaching of James pulls no punches:

---

46 Job 1:13-19.

47 Acts 6–7.

48 Acts 14:19.

Consider it pure joy, my brothers and sisters, whenever you face trials of many kinds, because you know that the testing of your faith produces perseverance.

(James 1:2-3)

And:

Brothers and sisters, as an example of patience in the face of suffering, take the prophets who spoke in the name of the Lord. As you know, we count as blessed those who have persevered. You have heard of Job's perseverance and have seen what the Lord finally brought about. The Lord is full of compassion and mercy.

(James 5:10-11)

Many of the first apostles, just like Stephen, were executed and died violent deaths, way before completing their 'natural life span'. It didn't mean God was angry with them. It didn't mean they died prematurely because their faith was too weak. They didn't die because of any personal inadequacies or sinful choices.

These are all examples of extraordinary people of faith who had bad things happen to them.

What made us think that good Christians don't experience bad stuff?

In John 10:10 Jesus tells us: 'The thief comes only to steal and kill and destroy; I have come that they may have life, and have it to the full.' What does it mean to have life to the full?

Interestingly Jesus did not expand in that passage on what life to the full means. He was teaching his disciples to follow his voice as the Good Shepherd to find salvation.

Before losing my wife, I tended to interpret this verse of Scripture as a simple binary thing. A life of blessing, health and prosperity are from the Lord. Death, loss and destruction are the work of the thief, the devil.

I now have a different interpretation of what Jesus said.

We know a life without love is not a full life. In the same way, a life full of pain and loss is not a full life. The reality is that loss is normal. Deep loss is the flipside of deep love. And the only way to avoid deep and grievous loss in life is not to love deeply.

If the Son of God experienced sorrow and grief, what makes us think we should be exempt from sorrow and grief?

Life to the full is a life encompassing love and blessing *and* sorrow and grief. Not either-or but and-and. Without both ends of the spectrum, life is incomplete and only lived partially.

As my friend Andrew said to me: 'I've never met a 150-year-old Christian. Or one who didn't age. Even those with healing ministries get sick and die.'

Loss and death are normal in life. We need to face up to them and learn how to deal with them.

Dragon 2: Caring for ourselves is selfish

In chapter 22 of the book of Matthew, Jesus is tested by a Sadducee expert in the law, who asks him, 'Teacher, which is the greatest commandment in the Law?' Note that the expert in the Law asked for one commandment, the greatest, but Jesus replied with two. He answered:

'Love the Lord your God with all your heart and with all your soul and with all your mind.' This is the first and greatest commandment. And the second is like it: 'Love your neighbour as yourself.' All the Law and the Prophets hang on these two commandments.
(Matthew 22:36-40)

Likewise, when the wealthy young man in Matthew 19 asked him which commandments he should keep, the last one he mentioned was 'love your neighbour as yourself' (v. 19). It's not a new one for the New Testament but he is quoting from the Old Testament book of Leviticus, 19:18.

Let's have another look at the second of the two commandments.

In the 2,500-plus sermons I have heard over the course of time, lots have focused on the first three words of the commandment. We are taught to love our neighbour and to lay down our lives for our brothers and sisters. We are taught to serve one another and place others above ourselves. This is all true and sound doctrine. But it's only a partial reading of the Scripture.

How about we examine the whole verse and focus on the fourth and fifth words? Love your neighbour *as yourself*. Check out the logic with me here. Does it mean that if we neglect and hate ourselves, we are to neglect and hate our neighbour in equal measure – *as ourselves*? Of course not. Does it say that we are to love our neighbour more than ourselves? I cannot find a single translation of the Bible that says that: they are all consistent in commanding us to love our neighbour as or as much as we love ourselves.

Sticking with the logic, that must mean that we are intended to love ourselves. If we don't love ourselves, how can we love our neighbour? And how can we love ourselves if we don't care for ourselves?

I realised early in the journey as Vicky's carer the importance of caring for myself in body, spirit and soul *so that* I could care for Vicky over the long run. I had heard of so many carers breaking down with exhaustion, to the point of needing care themselves, that I knew I would not be doing anyone any favours if I allowed that to happen in my case. My family were concerned enough about my welfare as well as Vicky's, so that I could not allow myself to become yet another exhausted and broken carer where someone else had to lay down their life to care for me ahead of time.

The church has taught us that our bodies are 'temples of the Holy Spirit' in the context of sexual immorality and that I am to honour God with my body (1 Corinthians 6:18-20). I have been taught the things I should avoid, I have been taught how to look after myself spiritually, and I have been taught not to be selfish, self-indulgent or vain. I have been taught about Sabbath rest and abstaining from work at least one day a week. In contrast, I have never been taught in church about the importance of taking care of my emotions or how to look after my body and soul. Why have we left self-care up to the self-help gurus in mainstream media and print to train us in these critical lifestyle issues?

How many great-hearted Christian workers, whether volunteers or staff, are burnt out by missions or churches who pay low regard to their physical and mental welfare? That of course is a whole different book for someone to write, but it reflects a mission mindset and culture where self-sacrifice is not only encouraged but it is *expected*. A late friend of mine was a trustee of a major international Christian charity. Her big question to the board of trustees was: 'How many of your workers come home on stretchers?' She meant the question both figuratively and literally.

All too often we can find mission-based cultures that pay scant regard to employment law that is designed to protect the welfare of workers, because employment law is regarded as 'secular' whereas the Lord's work is 'spiritual' and sacrificial. This attitude conveniently expresses the illusion of the sacred-secular divide – the belief that there is a division between sacred and secular dimensions in God's creation.[49]

Experience from leading bereavement courses quickly showed me how many Christians pay little attention to themselves in situations of bereavement. They believe their task is to take care of others and ignore their care for themselves and their own emotions of grief. They live out the commandment to love their neighbours but forget the two words 'as yourself' mean that they also have to look after themselves, care for themselves and allow themselves to grieve *so that* they can love others.

Let me be clear. I am not encouraging selfishness, self-indulgence or personal vanity. I am encouraging self-care as integral to pastoral care, *so that* we can care for others. I am encouraging the teaching of self-care by the church as an essential aspect of the Christian life if we are in it for the long run.

In short, I am encouraging us to see and apply all five words in the commandment: 'Love your neighbour as yourself.' Not just words one to three.

Dragon 3: Emotions are an attack of the devil

I often think we give the devil too much credit for what happens in our lives. Please don't misinterpret me as understating the reality of spiritual attack and warfare, but our conditioning can lead us to think negative emotions are symptoms of weakness, a failure of faith, or an attack of the devil. We are taught not to be led by our emotions but by our faith, and we can think that negative emotions are symptoms of spiritual attack. If we can think instead that our emotions are part of God's design for us, we can use them as data and information on what is happening to us at any specific time.

Let's get back to biblical basics.

---

49 See Mark Greene's excellent booklet *The Great Divide* (London: London Institute of Contemporary Christianity), 2010.

Imago Dei

A fundamental tenet of the Judeo-Christian faith is that we are made in God's image. This doesn't mean we are created as little gods, but we are made in the pattern of God's image.

Genesis 1:26 tells us that God made humankind 'in our image'. We believe we are made in the triune image of God: Father, Son and Holy Spirit. The fifth chapter of Genesis contains the genealogy from Adam to Noah. It begins:

> This is the written account of Adam's family line. When God created mankind, he made them in the likeness of God. He created them male and female and blessed them. And he named them 'Mankind' when they were created.
> (Genesis 5:1-2)

Just in case of any lingering doubt on the Imago Dei theme, when God blesses Noah immediately after the flood, God says to Noah: 'Whoever sheds human blood, by humans shall their blood be shed; for in the image of God has God made mankind' (Genesis 9:6).

On top of the affirmations about God creating humankind in his own image, Psalm 139 tells us:

> For you created my inmost being; you knit me together in my mother's womb. I praise you because I am fearfully and wonderfully made; your works are wonderful, I know that full well.
> (vv. 13-14)

God made us with the full plethora of our emotions, utterly amazing things called brains and he clothed us with bodies – temples of the Holy Spirit – as well as our spirits. And this is true for every man, woman and child in existence. People of faith and no faith alike understand every human being is made up of this complicated concoction of body, soul and spirit. Three in one. Our souls include our emotions, our powers of reason and our will – our ability to choose.

While Christian teaching recognises the interdependence of body, spirit and soul, the prevailing tradition is that our reason, our emotions and our bodies represent the 'self-life' as though they were something separate from our spiritual lives, that there is no good thing in what is described as our 'flesh life'.

My question is why God would 'fearfully and wonderfully' make us with bodies and souls as well as spirits if he thought the body and soul were superfluous 'flesh' to be disregarded?

I venture to think that if God made us in his image, as the book of Genesis so powerfully asserts, and he made us fearfully and wonderfully, that means he gave us bodies and souls as well as spirits for a reason that is more than simply to subjugate them.

I suggest that in the same way that the triune God of Father, Son and Holy Spirit work together in the mysterious dance of the Trinity, we humans are made of body, spirit and soul to dance the same wonderful and mysterious dance. A dance where all the inseparable parts of ourselves play their full role in glorifying God.

Do we need a new theology that embraces and cares for the whole person – in body, spirit and soul? I think that's what Jesus meant when he said in John 10:10 that he came so that we would have life to the full. Not denial of any dimension of life. Life to the full.

Our emotions are an integral part of us. Experiencing emotions is not a human design error or a bit of faulty wiring.

There is a big difference between being led by our emotions and being informed by them. We are not meant to be ruled by our emotions, but they play a big part in who we are and reflect how we are experiencing the world. They give us data that we can turn into information to help us navigate the world in which we live. They give us the 'gut feeling' that something is right or wrong, regardless of the apparent facts.

When 'Jesus wept' at the tomb of Lazarus (John 11:35), it was a display of his humanity and emotions for the grieving family and friends.

Emotional intelligence enables us not only to understand our own emotions but also to pick up on the emotions of others. In everyday life, my emotions give me data about how I am reacting to what is going on within and around me, and they help me make choices about how I will react. They help me navigate through normal life in a healthy (or unhealthy) way.

I found that grievous loss, however, is not the normal routine of life, and my emotions started to affect me in ways I could not have foreseen. I was neither educated nor trained to expect my emotions to disable me for normal life, even temporarily. I had to learn the hard way, often through private conversations in hushed tones from friends who had gone ahead of me in their own experiences of grief and could clearly recognise what I was going through. Those conversations helped me understand I wasn't an emotional wreck or failure, but how normal it was to experience such extreme emotions.

Let's explore this a bit further by checking out a few foundational scriptures. The apostle Paul wrote in the book of Romans:

> Don't you know that all of us who were baptised into Christ Jesus were baptised into his death? We were therefore buried with him through baptism into death in order that, just as Christ was raised from the dead through the glory of the Father, we too may live *a new life*.
> (Romans 6:3-4, emphasis mine)

In the letter to the Colossians, Paul wrote:

> Do not lie to each other, since you have taken off the old self with its practices and have put on *the new self*, which is being renewed in knowledge in the image of its Creator.
> (Colossians 3:9-10, emphasis mine)

In the letter to the Ephesians, we find the same reference to 'the new self':

> You were taught, with regard to your former way of life, to put off the old self, which is being corrupted by its deceitful desires; and to be made new in the attitude of your minds; and to put on *the new self*, created to be like God in true righteousness and holiness.
> (Ephesians 4:22-24, emphasis mine)

In his second letter to the church in Corinth, Paul wrote:

> Therefore, if anyone is in Christ, the new creation has come: the old has gone, the new is here!
> (2 Corinthians 5:17)

The Greek term for 'new self' is *neos anthropos* and it:

> Depicts an individual, male or female, who possesses a 'new nature' or 'new humanity.' It characterizes a metamorphosis in conduct from a life of sin to one of righteousness and is equivalent in meaning to being born again.[50]

And here's the point. When I became a Christian, the Bible tells me I was given a new life and a *new self*. I became a new creation. My new self is a new nature, a new humanity. That new humanity includes everything, not just my spirit. It is not only my spirit that is made new, but also my whole self: body, spirit and soul. That includes my emotional life and my thought life. The whole deal.

When I grieved, it was my new self who grieved. When my emotions overwhelmed me, they were the emotions of my new self and not my old self. To be honest, being a pretty rational kind of bloke, I had no experience of being overwhelmed by my emotions before I became a Christian, so how could this sense of overwhelming emotion be my old self in play?

All that tells me that it simply doesn't make biblical sense to think our emotions are just the devil's playground. They are part and parcel of who we are as human beings in Christ.

When we are made new, it is the whole of us that is made new, not just the spiritual dimension of our lives. Of course, it takes conscious effort to realign the way we think and behave, but the amazing thing is that we can rewire our brains and habits through practise and adopting new disciplines to walk the talk of our new selves.

Dragon 4: Church leaders know what to do

Leaders are all-knowing and all-seeing founts of wisdom who know just what to do and say at the right time in every situation, right?

It isn't just in churches that leaders become demi-gods whose every word is pored over to harvest their wisdom. The same applies in the worlds of

---

50 www.biblestudytools.com/dictionaries/bakers-evangelical-dictionary/new-self.html (accessed 1.12.23).

politics and business. Many people aspire to leadership and are seduced by the glitz, glamour and power in the title, the platform, holding audiences in thrall to their every word, the ambition and the sense of authority and power it will give them. Finally they have their chance to show the world where the answers lie, that they were right all along and the world will be so much better a place under their wise leadership.

Well, that's what leaders who are delusional sociopaths and narcissists think. Normal leaders don't think that way.

Anyone with experience of leadership in any sphere who has an ounce of emotional intelligence will tell you leadership can be one of the loneliest places on the planet. The love and support of a great family and friends helps, but it can never dilute the personal accountability of leaders for their organisations – and I include church leaders here. The responsibilities can be overwhelming. The decisions can be complex and deeply affect people's lives. They know the slightest slip of the tongue or mistake on their part will be scrutinised and chewed over endlessly by critics on the sidelines who know better but have never had the experience of being an accountable leader.

Genuine leaders experience opposition. They will tell you that their followers often have unrealistic expectations of their power and abilities to meet their needs. They will tell you their most valuable learning has resulted from their mistakes. The bigger the mistake, the greater the learning. Leaders sink or swim through how they learn or fail to learn. The choice is either to grow through learning, to duck, dive and muddle on, or to retrench and withdraw.

How do I know? I learned the hard way. These insights are not from textbooks on leadership, they are from my life experience ranging from leading large organisations to small faith-based groups and networks of people for more than thirty-five years in public services, the charitable sector and in business. I was a chief executive in the NHS for twelve years, with accountability for the healthcare services to large populations in organisations employing up to 4,000 staff. I have been pilloried in the press for contentious changes I have led. I have had a Guy Fawkes doll with my name around the neck in a meeting room, and my name in front of an empty chair on the speakers' platform of a packed meeting in a church hall where the organisers failed to invite me. I have had my (unflattering) caricature on the front page of a newspaper for two consecutive weeks. I have been the subject of malicious rumour and speculation. I have had sleepless nights worrying over important decisions, with incomplete information that I knew would impact people's lives and livelihoods.

Does that sound like fun?

It's no different leading a church or a ministry. The thing that is different is the vocational call, but the call to leadership is the same.

All leaders are human beings. All human beings are incomplete. *Ergo,* all leaders, including church leaders, are incomplete. It simply isn't possible for them to know the answer to everything or to understand completely life through the eyes and ears of their constituency. This is especially so when they have not experienced what their 'followers' have experienced. It verges on spiritual arrogance to believe otherwise.

So what?

I'm advocating three things to help blow up this illusory dragon of all-knowing leaders.

1. Training and education about loss

In the *Faith Questions* video of the brilliant Bereavement Journey course[51] initiated by Holy Trinity Brompton Church in London, Revd Yvonne Richmond Tulloch tells her story of regularly conducting funerals and ministering to the bereaved, answering their questions about God and death, before she lost her husband in his mid-forties. She tells of how her husband's death made her question her own faith, but how her bereavement and grief led her to better serve her parishioners with genuine empathy and understanding. Her training as a priest had equipped her to conduct rituals and share her theological insights into death, but her experience of sudden bereavement had fundamentally transformed how she related to the bereaved.

Don't get me wrong, I'm not advocating a cull of church leaders' spouses or close families so they can empathise with the bereaved in their churches or ministries. Or that churches and ministries only appoint leaders who have experienced deep grief. I think there are practical solutions that are somewhat kinder and less extreme. I'm advocating for the training and

---

51 www.thebereavementjourney.org/ (accessed 1.12.23).

education of church leaders and their congregations in dealing with loss in the church.

We have established that the experience of grief in bereavement shares many similarities to the experience of grief in losing a marriage through divorce, a job, a future hope, a home through repossession, an intimate friendship or relationship. All of these grievous losses can trigger extreme emotions, shame, guilt and self-doubt, they can undermine a person's identity and faith. And that's the stuff of real life that goes on below the surface of church if the teaching and preaching focuses exclusively on the evangelical and missional call of Christianity. And it's the stuff of real life in the villages, towns and cities the church is called to serve. That's where the rubber hits the road, and where the missional teaching and preaching can come alive in a society that is not well served in handling matters of deep loss.

2. Helping leaders understand they are incomplete

I'm advocating for an understanding among leaders that they are incomplete in their experience, gifts, skills, learning and education. I would go further and say they will always be incomplete, no matter how much they learn. That is not to discourage learning and education; it is to encourage a wise humility in leaders to know they cannot be the answer to everything. The reality is they will burn out if they try to be everything to everyone.

There is deep wisdom in leaders knowing their own incompleteness, and gathering around them people who have the gifts, skills and experience they lack. Isn't that what five-fold ministry is all about: 'Christ himself gave the apostles, the prophets, the evangelists, the pastors and teachers' (Ephesians 4:11).

No single person in church leadership has the whole kit bag. They may have more than one gift, but never the lot. Leaders need other leaders, not as competitors or rivals, but to complement the gifts of the leader with different gifts.

Regardless of their gift, a church leader still carries the spiritual accountability before God for their church, but they do not have to be responsible to do everything. The job of teaching and educating the church in handling loss is the job of teachers. The job of ministering to people suffering loss is the job of pastors.

The job of the church leader in this context is threefold:

- Firstly, to ensure the teaching, education and ministry get done.
- Secondly, to develop their personal skills in how to listen and respond to people experiencing loss.
- Thirdly, to point them to the people who can help if they can't.

'I'll pray for you' is a well-meaning but partial and inadequate response.

It can be incredibly liberating for leaders who genuinely understand this idea of their own incompleteness and the limits of their own humanity. For leaders wishing to explore this idea more, the *Harvard Business Review* published a fabulous article in February 2007 entitled 'In Praise of the Incomplete Leader'.[52] I wished it had been published twenty years earlier. When I read it in 2007, I think I grew two inches taller as so much weight fell off my shoulders.

3. Christians need to understand their leaders are human too

Christians in the wider church, congregations and parishioners, need to understand their leaders are human and incomplete too. They are not necessarily equipped to help their issues – they can pray and gain spiritual insight but people experiencing grievous loss need whole-person care.

Whole-person care is the job of the wider church as well as the leadership. It means wanting to learn to help those in pain from grievous loss. It means learning to avoid the spiritual bypass of 'I'll pray for you' when we just don't know what to say or do. Don't misunderstand me, I am not devaluing or denigrating genuine offers of prayer. I recall well a friend in church leadership not only offering to pray about the situation with Vicky but asking me *how* she should pray and *what* to pray – I really appreciated that sense of wanting to align her prayer with mine and to be specific.

---

52 https://hbr.org/2007/02/in-praise-of-the-incomplete-leader (accessed 1.12.23).

Learning to help those in pain is at the heart of this book. It's really quite simple and it's all about the way we behave:

- Be present for them – don't avoid them.
- Hear them and see them – don't try and fix them.
- Make them feel safe – don't judge them, gossip about them or assume you know what is going on for them.
- Ask how you can pray for them – don't offer spiritual platitudes.

You won't go far wrong if you follow those simple do's and don'ts.

Dragon 5: Cake is not the only answer

To finish on a lighter note. And by the way, you can blame my friend Rachel for this one. Have you ever noticed how much cake is consumed by people offering comfort to those in trouble? Tea and cake seem to be a popular default. I don't mean to sound miserly, but it strikes me (and Rachel) that it is rather odd that we default to administering a refined sugar rush, an addictive substance proven to be harmful to our health, when we wouldn't dream of offering a cigarette, a whisky or a snort of cocaine to dull the pain.

Tea, on the other hand, has well proven benefits for our mental health. Just saying.

And here is another of life's paradoxes …

Do I eat and enjoy cake? You bet I do. Did I accept the offer of cake when I was grieving? You bet I did. Am I saying don't offer tea and cake? No. Just don't think they are magic bullets to take the pain away.

Time to reflect

Please take a few minutes now to reflect on what you have read in this chapter. Here are some more questions to prompt you:

- Have you ever found yourself denying your emotions in grief and thinking you are failing in your faith?

- Do you take time intentionally to look after yourself when you are charged with the care of others?
- Does it ever occur to you that your leaders are human, just like you?

Chapter Seven: The Beginning of Loss

All people are like grass … The grass withers and the flowers fall,
because the breath of the Lord blows on them. Surely the people
are grass. The grass withers and the flowers fall, but the word of our
God endures for ever.
(Isaiah 40:6-8)

In this chapter I'm going deeper into the story of Vicky's journey with
dementia and our experience.

Not every death is from dementia, but I hope you will stick with the
story as the more general insights may be helpful as you navigate your
story, whatever your circumstances might be.

The early signs

The trouble with so many degenerative or progressive diseases and conditions is that we never know when they start. As carers and family members,
we beat ourselves up wondering if things would have been different if we
had done something about it earlier. I know that sense of underlying guilt
will resonate with many carers for loved ones with progressive conditions.

My family and I have tried to figure out the timeline for the onset of
Vicky's dementia, trying to trace back the changes in her character and
behaviour over the previous decade with only approximate success. We
haven't done so thinking we could have changed anything, but more to
process and understand our gradual loss.

I can't claim my attempt to build a picture of the chronology and progression of Vicky's condition is an accurate attempt to describe the natural
progression of the condition, but maybe it can help others facing the

condition either for themselves or their loved ones or friends to understand better what's going on and how best to respond when you notice things changing in someone's character or developing habits that concern you.

Firstly, let me tell you a bit more about Vicky.

When we met in 1974, she was a strong-willed, socially confident, independently minded feminist who was also fully feminine, and happened to be gorgeous too. I already told you she stood me up on our first date to attend an exhibition in London without telling me she was going. She just left a message with a flatmate to tell me when I arrived to pick her up. Not the best start.

She became a loving and generous wife, mother and friend, always putting others ahead of herself and always ready to help. Nothing was too much trouble. She would lay down anything she was doing to help a friend in need. She was passionate about the marginalised and disadvantaged. She always took the side of the underdog. She hated injustice.

She was one of those annoying people who seem physically ageless – in her late fifties most people thought she was in her late thirties or early forties.

She was twenty years ahead of her time on issues like nutrition and organic food. I remember having to crawl around the lower shelves of supermarkets to scrutinise every additive in the food we bought in the early 1980s when manufacturers got away with specifying their ingredients in the small print on the labels, especially after our first daughter, Ali, was born. In the late 1980s, in the pre-www age, she searched out the few suppliers either locally or nationally of organic vegetables and meat. She was regarded by many as a food crank at the time, and she really didn't care. She knew what she thought was right and would stick to her guns.

She was clever, emotionally intelligent and creative – her paintings continue to decorate the walls of our house, and believe me, I'm picky when it comes to art, so this isn't just sentimentality.

I write this not to be misty-eyed and see the past as the 'golden days', but to get across the fact that degenerative conditions are indiscriminate – they can strike anyone and it's not their fault.

As we have tried to piece the story together, the common thread about Vicky's behaviour change was when her 'worldview' switched from being a passionate Christian faith into an obsessive preoccupation with the biblical

End Times – especially the rapture.[53] I'm not here to argue the rights and wrongs of interpretations on the subject itself. But I will warn against the very real dangers of pushing theological worldviews to the point they become obsessions either for oneself or for others. The fine line between faith-filled passion and tunnel-vision obsession must be carefully and responsibly guarded.

The alert balloon really went up when an older friend we had known for years asked me one Sunday morning at church, 'What's happened to our Vicky?' Her daughter was a psychiatrist and she had spotted over the course of several conversations that Vicky was repetitive and obsessive in talking to her – she thought she was 'regressing'. She took me aside and explained that regression was a sign of gradual loss of mental capacity that could continue all the way back to childhood, to the point of becoming a child in an adult's body.

I found it truly scary to hear that from a psychiatrist, but at the same time the explanation helped me understand some things I had observed in Vicky's behaviour over recent times. Sometime earlier I had been thinking that our relationship had been shifting from husband and wife as equals and partners to something more like husband and dependent wife, or father-daughter. She had started asking my permission to do things or asking me to do things that she had always done herself. I was perplexed why that might be happening. Was it me just thinking our relationship was changing – or was it really changing? I had noticed she had seemed unable to make quite simple choices of her own and started to ask me to make the choices for her. And now I had a possible explanation.

Her command of English had declined in quite subtle ways that only those very close to her could notice. She had started to say things like 'I did go' rather than 'I went', 'I did do' rather than 'I did'. But when anyone tried to correct her, she would say English was her fourth language: so a stranger or a new friend would think that for someone raised in Angola speaking Portuguese she had a remarkable fluency in English. She was indeed fully fluent in English, having British parents and an excellent honours degree from a 'red-brick' English university in 1978, despite a Portuguese education in Angola up until admission to university.

---

53 See 1 Thessalonians 4:17.

I tell this aspect of the story because she was so bright and intelligent that she had developed masking techniques to disguise her loss of language, mental capacity and memory. And here's a big insight. The fact that people may be losing their mental faculties doesn't make them suddenly unintelligent or dim. They are simply losing a part of their cognitive functioning, but not all of it. A part of their brain is dying, and the rest of it can be perfectly healthy and compensating for the part that is declining.

Another tell-tale sign was the gradual decline in the quality of her art. It had been a lifelong passion and, once the children had all left home, she was able to dedicate several hours a day to her work. Her best work was of a very high standard, and she had a special gift in bringing inanimate objects to life, especially buildings, painting them full of shade, light and character. She might complete a canvas or two in a week, and always sought my opinion. I knew what her best was like, and I tried to encourage her to match her best. But the point came when the light and shade started to diminish, would come back periodically and then diminish again. I was finding it ever more difficult to know how to praise and encourage her when her efforts at specific commissions for friends and family started to become more childlike, one-dimensional and on occasions almost cartoonish. Any suggestion for improvement was taken as personal criticism and drew a depressive reaction.

It got to the point where, towards the end of her time at home, I dreaded her asking me what I thought and yet I knew she hung on my approval. From one or two good and occasionally excellent canvases a week, she had started producing five or six simplistic, repetitive and one-dimensional canvases. I didn't feel I could lie and I tried to be as gentle as I could. In reality, I had no language or training as a carer to know how to handle this stuff when I knew Vicky's mood hung on my reactions. As with her loss of language, I only realised in hindsight that her loss of understanding of what I was saying was compensated by how she read my reaction and facial expressions rather than the words I used. She had always been able to read my reactions, and I wish I had understood then that it is OK to affirm the reality of someone experiencing harmless delusions in dementia by 'playing along'. After all, we do that with children, encouraging them to play and exercise their imaginations. And yet I thought it dishonest to deal in such a way with a fully grown, mature adult.

I could have done with some training on how to react in encouraging ways while staying true to myself.

Denial and clever compensation

Please understand the stories I tell here are not intended remotely to diminish Vicky as a person or violate her memory. They are shared to help shed some light on the insidious progression of degenerative conditions *and* try to sustain the dignity of the person living with the condition, regardless of their awareness.

For years Vicky denied there was anything wrong with her, and despite pleadings from me and our family she refused to engage with any professional support or help. As I was the only person she would talk to honestly, it meant I fell into a trap of trying to be her 'therapist' as well as her husband. And I was clearly not equipped for that.

Her closest family all thought she was mentally ill. As an intelligent woman, however, she was skilled in disguising publicly what was going on, and maintaining her personal dignity. She managed to frame her obsessional behaviour as spiritually passionate and prophetic.

My amateur attempts to help her through encouraging changes in her thinking, particularly around her sense of self-worth, seemed to have an effect, but only for a limited time. A pattern of thinking would seem to change and be broken, only to return after a few days. In all of this period I believed she still had some choices over how she thought about herself and her childhood especially, and it frustrated me that she would seem to change only then to revert and become defiant and refuse to recognise there was a problem.

The next noticeable stage was when she admitted to me to feeling depressed. I had thought that for some time, and that her admission was progress. But it came with a sting because she blamed me and her closest family for telling her she needed help – and therefore we were the ones making her feel depressed. She thought it was our fault and we should be encouraging her instead.

In the next breath she would declare that she was healed 'by the stripes of Jesus' and didn't need anyone's help. Which would have been a great position of faith to take if she didn't deny the need for healing in the first place. Ironic but deeply sad.

Understanding Vicky's emotions

Vicky's emotional responsiveness was the next thing to go. Or so it seemed. It was so puzzling and painful to see how, on occasions, she apparently no longer cared for the people or things she was usually so passionate about. And 'on occasions' is a big clue here. Because it was on occasions, not all the time.

I remember driving home from a work meeting one day and having a miraculous escape in my car as it aquaplaned in torrential rain on a roundabout on a dual carriageway. I ended up literally feet away from the oncoming traffic from the opposite direction, with the double whammy of facing the wrong way around the roundabout with the car engine stalled.

I got home around twenty minutes after my escapade and I was clearly in shock. I was so glad to be home and I immediately poured it all out to Vicky. And I met a complete blank. She said something like, 'Have you had a good day?' and then proceeded to tell me what she had been doing and went into the kitchen, asking what I wanted for supper. She clearly had no understanding at all of what had just happened to me, or how shaken I was.

On another occasion, on a Sunday afternoon in 2011, four years before her diagnosis and nine years before her death, our middle daughter, Sam, arrived unannounced from Southampton with her boyfriend, Matt.

They came in, eyes glistening with excitement, and I knew instinctively the purpose of the visit. Matt had already asked my permission to ask her to marry him. Vicky was reading emails on her laptop and didn't get up to greet them. No hugs for her daughter on her surprise visit was just plain weird. They sat on the sofa, and Sam proudly showed us her engagement ring. She was overjoyed. Vicky meanwhile stayed seated and responded by saying, 'That's lovely, darling, but come and look at this email I've received from Israel.' She showed no emotion at all. Poor Sam was devastated, looked at me and mouthed, 'Daddy, what's going on?' They had had such a close mother-daughter relationship and now, in Sam's moment of joy, her mother was no longer there for her emotionally. As we came to learn, it wasn't

Vicky's indifference to Sam or any disapproval of Matt. Nor was it her fault. Nonetheless, it was one of those unforgettable moments on the journey and it was deeply distressing and painful for us all.

On the surface it seemed like Vicky's emotional capacity had diminished. In retrospect I'm not sure she understood what Sam had told us in that moment, or the significance of the ring, and therefore didn't know how to respond. She knew a response of some kind was expected, and so she responded by asking Sam to look at an email she thought would interest her.

It took quite a while for me to understand the effect of dementia on the brain. I now liken it to a set of lights on a Christmas tree, where one bulb starts to flicker and die, but it's not obvious to any observer. And then another bulb flickers and dies, then another, until gradually the lights may still be on but the light they give off has dimmed, and the gaps between the bulbs are increasingly clear.

Depression sets in

I knew Vicky suffered bouts of depression, but it took several years (possibly 2012 or 2013) before she acknowledged her depression to me. She said it started because I had not agreed with her dream in 2009 that the world was about to come to an end that year or the next. Sadly, this kind of dream had been a regular feature of life for us over the preceding years to the point of obsession, and she was not amenable to any conversation about such dreams. In her mind they were prophetic, and that was that.

I share the point here that she blamed me for her condition not as any absolution for myself, but as one of the most distressing aspects of the condition that carers, particularly spouses and close family, must cope with and manage. The truth is that you question yourself and wonder what you could have done differently. Could I have been more supportive or affirming? Was I to blame for her depression, like she said? Did I have a completely delusional view of myself? Was I failing as a husband and father? I'm sure many carers will recognise it is genuinely very easy to beat ourselves up and feel guilty as failing partners when this kind of thing happens. Could I have done more?

And here's another point about the journey and reading the early signs of progressive disease, in this case, dementia. Something that had changed in Vicky over the prior and more recent years, well before we knew something was wrong with her mental health, were a number of subtle changes in her behaviour and character. As a mild example, she started saying openly to me and our family that I had always chosen where we lived and she had never had any choice about the houses we bought, or any control over our finances. It troubled me to think she saw me as so dominant and overbearing that I had taken away her choices, and I really started to question myself. I don't want to make out that I was the perfect husband, but it was only later, as her condition progressed, that I understood how her gradual loss of memory had changed the way she experienced our relationship. Nevertheless, the complaints started to increase and I had to check in with our daughters whether they had seen me behave in the ways Vicky was describing. Thankfully, they were able to reassure me.

It's easy retrospectively to recognise it was the degenerative nature of her condition that led to these behaviours and not beat myself up with guilt, but just thinking that she held me responsible for how she felt was another painful and quite brutal shift in our relationship. It felt like, in her eyes, we weren't a 'we' anymore but a 'him and me'.

Truth be told, the journey only got real definition on that awful day in December 2015. That was the day when the condition I had most feared, and whose possibility I had denied, was confirmed.

Vicky's insight

In so many ways I am thankful that Vicky had only a brief period of insight when she genuinely understood that her faculties were in decline.

In 2013 she seemed to stop blaming me for how depressed she was feeling, and had several deeply depressive episodes when she would ask me what was wrong with her. They were triggered by social occasions. On the first occasion, we had gone to a party with another couple, and on the return journey of more than an hour, Vicky and her friend hardly stopped talking to each other and laughing together. The following morning, Vicky was in tears telling me that she had not understood anything her friend had said to her. She knew something was seriously wrong.

That was followed a couple of months later by a Christmas party with friends where I could see she had no idea of what was happening in the crowded room. She had retreated to a corner and her eyes were full of confusion. She looked like a lost child who didn't know where she was, why or with whom. As we drove away, she again broke down in tears saying she hadn't understood anything anyone was saying, or why we were even there.

This may sound perverse, but the period of her insight was thankfully brief, as it spared her a lot of pain and anguish. The downside was that she reverted to denial that there was anything wrong and doubled down on blaming me and the family for exhorting her to seek help. She hated being told there was something wrong with her, so we had to change tack and set out to manage the situation rather than confront it, as confrontation only made it worse emotionally and mentally for her.

Managing the brutal reality

The brutal reality is that these shifts in behaviour can happen slowly with dementia and are almost unnoticeable when they happen. They mount up gradually and insidiously, which is why I think practical illustrations of the underlying change of character and capability might help others reflect on behaviour changes they may be seeing in loved ones.

I will give one further example here because it goes to the heart of how difficult it can be for a carer, even before they realise they are a carer, to safeguard a loved one's welfare and personal dignity.

I have made the point previously about Vicky's strong character, determination and independence as well as her overriding kindness and generosity. She didn't need the feminist movement of the 1970s to liberate her as a woman. She had already learned that as a young white woman in Angola battling against racial prejudice and sexism. Friends from her youth in Angola have shared many stories with me about how Vicky was the 'icon of cool' and feminism in their culture. Being white helped her, of course, to express her countercultural radicalism in Portuguese colonial Africa, but my point here is about the depth of her character and conviction. And while it seems pretty basic to write this in the 2020s, I had to work out at this pre-diagnosis stage that the guarantors of her sense of autonomy were now limited to five things: her car, her sat nav to get places in her car, her personal bank account, her freedom to paint and her mobile phone. What I had spotted, however, was that Vicky had stopped being able to take on and learn new things or adapt to changes in technology. That meant only two of those five things – her car and her freedom to paint – were not subject to technological changes to which she would need to adapt. And the adaptation issues were compounded by the regressive nature of her condition, which meant she was becoming gradually more childlike and unlearning old things rather than learning new things.

Effectively she was stuck in an earlier world understanding of how, most specifically, the business of personal finance had changed from local branch banking to telephone and online banking. In practice, she found the shift to online and telephone banking virtually impossible to navigate alone and she had become ever more dependent on me for support to do what she wanted to do.

To make the point clearly in both its personal and social application, Vicky had become, unknowingly to me and unwittingly for her, an easy target for financial fraud. Her vulnerability only became clear one day when she was with her friend Liz at home and the phone rang. Vicky answered, left the phone off the hook, came back with her cheque book and started reading out all her account details to the caller. Fortunately, Liz overheard her, stopped her in mid-flow and made her put the phone down.

Vicky had no understanding of why she couldn't give 'the nice man on the phone' her bank details. She had worked in a bank for several years after we got married and knew the dangers of fraud. The brutal reality was that in her regression she had gained a childlike naivety that took everything at face value and was upset that she had not been allowed to give the 'nice man' her bank details. Liz told me about the episode, and I reinforced the explanation about not giving her bank details to anyone at all because of the possibility of fraud. It was apparent, however, that she now had no understanding of what I meant by fraud or stealing, or why anyone would want to take her money away from her.

On another occasion we were walking to the shops, and she insisted on crossing the road and seemed very anxious. After we had crossed over, she kept glancing across to the other side and dodging behind parked cars as if to avoid being seen. I couldn't get her to tell me why she was ducking up and down between the cars, but it dawned on me that she was trying to hide from someone.

The truth came out a few days later when she told me that a man she had met on the high street had come to our front door one day and took her to the nearest ATM to take out £250 for him and his family. I then discovered that hadn't been the first time.

My point is that Vicky, at that stage of a condition we did not understand and could not name, was highly vulnerable to fraud and theft. And while I knew this was an invasion of her privacy, I had to start opening and checking her bank statements to see if any other unusual transactions had taken place. And sure enough, I found multiple monthly standing orders she had set up in response to phone calls or street campaigners for 'compassionate causes'. Thankfully, none of them were illegitimate, but equally when asked about them, she had agreed because they were 'nice men' (virtually always men – sorry, fellas!) who needed money and had a sob story to tell. The reality was that she had lost the ability to engage intelligently with the world of finance. And I couldn't do a thing about it because I had no standing whatsoever with her bank – rightly, of course, in terms of protecting her assets – but frustratingly nonetheless when I knew she was being exploited.

How did I respond? I had to resort to simple underhand deception. Take this as one of those things carers may have to do to safeguard their loved ones. We didn't have any Powers of Attorney in place and I was therefore legally powerless to stop my wife being defrauded. I knew she was mentally impaired yet we had no clinical diagnosis to back up what we all knew in the family, but which Vicky vigorously denied. Catch 22.

Ironically, this is where her inability to engage with telephone and online banking came to the rescue. I had set up her security details and passwords in the first place and written them down for her (I know, I know – another one for the charge sheet!). As a subterfuge I simply had to 'forget', or not try too hard to remember, her security details and passwords or where she kept them so she couldn't access her account or pay for anything either online or over the phone.

To be candid, I really struggled with starting to use subterfuge to keep her safe against her expressed will. When you have shared a life of complete mutual trust, that's a very hard thing to start to do. In hindsight, I take comfort from knowing it can be kinder to play along with the memories and delusions of people with dementia rather than contradict and deny the reality they are experiencing in the moment. It's their reality, and why disturb it if they are safe and happy in that reality?

Uncertainty and helplessness

The emotions I experienced in the five or six years prior to Vicky's diagnosis were a complete maelstrom – a restless, stressful, disordered and tumultuous state of affairs. I was confused and uncertain. I was uncertain because I didn't know what we were dealing with, or how or when it would conclude.

I went through a period of denial of the possibility of dementia as I reasoned Vicky was too young for such a condition. I clung on to the healing scriptures and prayed endlessly for her to be well. I guess deep inside I also dreaded the possibility of her not recovering but declining to a slow and painful death over the many years when she should have been in her prime. I didn't want to admit the possibility that our plans for the future were now evaporating before my very eyes, regardless of our faith.

The result was that I held on to the hope of finding the solution, the right treatment that could bring her back to normal, to being the wife, mother and now grandmother we all so loved. As she would not accept help from the medical profession, I was constantly trying in my amateur way to 'treat' her and find some kind of breakthrough.

I was holding on to a hope that I could help her to recover. I took on myself a burden of responsibility for her to get better and be healed because she did not seem able to take that responsibility herself and refused to let anyone else help. In reality, it was a false hope that made me feel even more helpless to help her recover.

Keeping Vicky safe

In the midst of the maelstrom, I had to take on the responsibility to keep her safe.

Throughout this pre-diagnosis period, Vicky had started to lose her sense of social inhibition in ways that either caused social embarrassment or even placed her potentially in danger. She would start running in the streets in winter when we were out walking in coats and wellies with the dog. She would try to lift family and friends physically off their feet because she thought it was fun. She would stop strangers in the street and start praying for them without any prior conversation, their consent or any context for prayer. She would try to hug people she had never met before. While they might have been embarrassing, they were the relatively harmless things I saw happening when she was with me.

More potentially dangerous was my discovery that she had invited male strangers into our house so she could show them her paintings and give them away. She told me about an incident when she was really pleased the young man passing by our house had come in and accepted one of her paintings. We talked about it and I told her she must not invite strange men into the house if I wasn't home. She appeared to accept what I said but then ignored me completely. I found out because a male neighbour told me she had invited him in to see her paintings and he had felt distinctly uncomfortable knowing that she didn't recognise him or know his name, and yet was inviting him into our house when she was alone, calling him darling and asking him to take one of her paintings.

To the outside world, Vicky must have seemed like an engaging and sociable, if slightly eccentric person, who said encouraging and lovely things to women like, 'You're so beautiful', which was one of her devices to connect with someone while masking the fact that she didn't understand what people were saying back to her. It was like the 'receivers' in her brain had degraded faster than her 'transmitters', but she knew a response might be expected and so she would make one of a limited number of statements she used regularly rather than give relevant responses to the comments made.

This all created a real dilemma for me. How could I keep her safe *and* not restrict her freedom even to open the door to people at home? Later on, once we had the diagnosis, I knew the journey ahead with dementia could be many years and I didn't want to make our home so much of a fortress that she couldn't even go into the garden to feed the birds, or take the dog for a walk. She would have resented that deeply and she was so resourceful even in her declining mental capacity that she would have found a way out anyway.

To all intents and purposes, we were facing many years when her faculties had been slowly declining, and my decisions had to be based on a simple judgement about the level of risk we could reasonably take to maintain her enjoyment of life and sense of freedom and autonomy. I decided I would rather she enjoyed the remaining life she had in the home she loved rather than minimise all risks and attempt to restrict her movements completely.

My big takeaway from this experience is that however much I wanted to change the way Vicky thought and behaved, I really had no power over her choices. I could try to persuade or cajole her to think differently, but I couldn't do it for her.

Everything within me wanted to rescue her. And I carried guilt that I could not rescue her. I could only love and protect her as best I could.

Time to reflect

Time for another pause and some more questions.

- Have you ever noticed yourself taking on responsibility to 'fix' someone's behaviour and 'rescue' them when you have seen things that trouble you?
- Have you taken on a sense of guilt when a loved one's behaviour has changed for the worse?
- Have you ever felt guilty for playing along with someone's delusional reality when they are mentally compromised?

Chapter Eight: Lost and Found – the Diagnosis

Our journey took on real and devastating definition on 15 December 2015. That was the awful day when the condition I had most feared, and the possibility I had denied, was confirmed.

Vicky was diagnosed with probable frontotemporal dementia (FTD) in an out-patient clinic by a consultant psychiatrist. And while the consultant's diagnosis of FTD was only 'probable', the definitive aspect was her statement that there was no treatment to improve, alleviate, or even delay the condition.

The consultant was empathetic and caring. I was speechless and genuinely devastated. I had denied the possibility of dementia, reasoning Vicky was too young, and up to that point I had clung to the hope that her condition was a treatable mental illness.

Vicky's diagnosis was the point where grief really kicked in. The shock of the diagnosis and the brutality of the prognosis of an unremitting decline in my wife's health simply wrecked me. Even though she was still with me, I started to grieve for losing the wife I loved while she was still living and breathing and physically present. I felt helpless to help her.

In the light of my later experience of grief at her death, I now think of this experience as my first cycle of grief. I thought it was preparing me for the grief to follow with her seemingly inevitable death, but I now see it as a cycle of grief in its own right that prepared me *in part* for a second cycle of grief with her death.

For some weeks I was incapable of concentrating at work. I might have been at work physically, but my mind and emotions were simply overwhelmed by the enormity of the diagnosis and what we were now facing, and who knew for how long? There was very little literature on FTD simply because there had been no real investment in research. What sparse research there was gave a maximum life prognosis of ten years, but even that was unclear if the prognosis was from onset or diagnosis. And we had no real idea when the FTD had taken root, other than trying to piece together the chronology of her behaviour change from our collective memories. In reality, we had very little to go on. But her death suddenly felt very close and imminent.

The diagnosis was devastating for our children and for Vicky's siblings at multiple levels. It not only painted a brutal picture of her future for them but, given she was a very young sixty-one, it raised all sorts of questions about the cause of her condition and whether there was a genetic predisposition in her side of the family.

The family research function went into frantic overdrive. The results were inconclusive because there was so little understanding of the condition at the time. At the time of writing, eight years after Vicky's diagnosis, the Alzheimer's Research UK booklet *What is Frontotemporal Dementia?* indicates that for behavioural variant FTD 'one in every two or three people with the disease could have a family history', while: 'In cases of FTD where there is no family history, the risk factors for the disease are not yet fully understood. Because FTD is a rarer type of dementia it is harder for researchers to study its causes.'[54] Thankfully, we were able to discount the familial possibility, as none of us could think of any relatives in Vicky's family line who had contracted dementia. The reality, however, was that her diagnosis had the effect of triggering multiple additional anxieties in the family that took several months of research and painful conversations to put in perspective.

In the event, Vicky lived for a little over four years after the diagnosis, and with the help of friends and family, we were able to care for her at home for all but the last nine months of her life.

Ironically, the only person seemingly unaffected by the diagnosis was Vicky herself. Despite the clarity of the message, Vicky became even more determined in her refusal to accept there was anything wrong. She insisted it was now the doctor's fault for making her feel depressed and negative about herself. She refused to accept that she would now lose her driving licence as the doctor would have to notify the DVLA of her incapacity to drive.

---

54 www.alzheimersresearchuk.org/dementia-information/types-of-dementia/frontotemporal-dementia (accessed 13.12.23).

If there was any upside to her denial about her dementia it was that she had no insight into what it meant. She was angry that the consultant said she would not be allowed to drive and insisted I should let her drive regardless. And while I was suddenly off the hook for making her feel depressed, I was now between a rock and a hard place for having to be the enforcer of the requirement that she could no longer drive.

In many respects, her car had been her lifeline to combat her sense of isolation and affirm her sense of purpose. Even though I worked from home, I was so absorbed by business in the daytime that I failed to recognise her loneliness until some years later. I still saw her as I had known her all our lives together, as a self-starting and independently minded person. It's easy to think with hindsight that I should have noticed this, that or the other sign of her progressive decline. But suddenly the new scrapes, scratches and dents that appeared every few months on her car, and which she couldn't explain, took on a new light and started to make sense.

Vicky was adamant she was able to drive. Trying to explain that she was disqualified from driving and was no longer insurable had no effect whatsoever. She had no understanding of either of those concepts. She had no insight that she was now a danger to herself and others on the roads. That meant my new task was to find a way of stopping her from driving while also hoping she would not blame me this time for taking her car away.

In the short term, it meant I had to offer to take her everywhere she wanted to go so that she didn't feel her freedom to travel had been taken away. Reasonable enough, you might say, but it didn't solve the underlying problem, which was that she could get in the car and drive off at any time it suited her. That meant I had to play the long game, and I'm not proud of this but I started by hiding her house and car keys while waiting on a more permanent solution to emerge.

Thankfully, my sister and her family came to visit and managed 'to borrow' Vicky's sat nav, which she had always depended on to go anywhere, and that gave us a little breathing space as a family to find a longer-term solution Vicky would accept. In retrospect, it was another shift in our relationship that had already gone from husband to carer and was now travelling in the territory of parent to child, where I had to limit the choices available to her to keep her safe.

If you are a carer for someone with dementia, I suspect you will know exactly what I mean. And if you haven't had to do it yet, don't agonise too much or beat yourself up when you know you are trying to act in the best interests of someone you love. I'm afraid to say we had to be 'inventive' repeatedly to negotiate life without devastating Vicky emotionally. It so happened our middle daughter, Sam, had a one-year-old toddler and was finding it increasingly difficult to get him in and out of her small car safely, so I asked Vicky if Sam could 'borrow' her car to help her out. She was reluctant but her generous maternal instincts kicked in and she consented, provided I bought her a new one if the doctor said she could drive again. The reality was that Vicky would not give up her car, regardless of the danger she posed to herself and other road users. Her car was a means of personal freedom and autonomy, but I could never have forgiven myself if she or someone else had been seriously injured because of my failure to act. It was hard enough for her to accept she couldn't drive, but if I had simply taken her car away, she would have been devastated. The result of our little family manipulation was that she understood she was helping our daughter and grandson, and while she missed her car, she knew it was serving a good cause.

Subsequently, every time we went to church together, we would drive past the garage where we had bought her car and without fail, she would ask me to stop and buy her a new one! I soon cottoned on that I had to change our driving routes to overcome that problem, and not to trigger her memory of the car she had lost. And sure enough, as her memory was triggered less, she started gradually to forget the loss of her car.

A strange new freedom

While the diagnosis of dementia was devastating, it proved to be strangely liberating. In our loss I had found something new. Let me explain.

The diagnosis helped me understand that Vicky wasn't behaving out of defiance or denial. The degenerative nature of her condition meant she just couldn't help thinking the way she did or seeing the world the way she did. I had been frustrated with what I thought was her refusal to accept what was happening, but now I understood it wasn't her fault. She wasn't being stubborn or defiant. She just could not help it.

That was when I started to marvel at her ingenuity and how clever she was, for example, at diverting attention away from her inability to understand what people were saying to her. She did this either by asking people to explain what they meant or by simply changing the subject and making a completely unrelated statement when she realised someone was awaiting a response to their question. Effectively her condition had advanced to where her 'send' mode of communication was still functioning but her 'receive mode' was severely impaired. She realised people were talking to her and expecting a response, so she made a response. Just not a relevant response.

Our understanding of the combination of the degenerative and regressive nature of the brain condition shed a completely different light on so many puzzling, hurtful and even amusing events of the previous years.

Both friends and family were burdened with guilt over the period before the diagnosis, asking whether they could have done or said something sooner. Our psychiatrist friend told me how she wished she had said something, but the reality is that nothing could have been done anyway as the condition was both degenerative and untreatable.

Guilt is a terrible burden to carry, especially when it is guilt at our perceived failure to do something we thought we could have done to change an outcome. In the Roman Catholic tradition of my childhood, it would be categorised as a 'sin of omission' where we fail to act when we could have changed a bad outcome. I recall vividly Vicky's personal sense of guilt over her brother's death when she thought it was in her power to do something that wasn't remotely in her power, and yet she carried the burden of it through the remainder of her life and could not forgive herself when there was nothing really to forgive. She could not have changed the outcome, and yet carried the guilt for her 'omission'. However much she was reassured by her family that there was nothing she could have done and didn't need to be forgiven, she was unable to forgive herself.

It's one of those awful dilemmas of life that we so often see and experience losses we mistakenly think we could have helped avoid. The results can be truly toxic to our mental health when there is no one to forgive us, basically because there is nothing to forgive, and yet we are unable to forgive ourselves.

My learning from the journey with Vicky was that it was painful enough having to deal with the brutal facts confronting us without adding feelings of guilt for events I could not have reasonably anticipated. Life was already stressful enough without blaming myself for things I could not control. I had to let go of the pretence of control.

I learned after the diagnosis that our daughter Sam,when she was training as a junior doctor, had been pretty certain that her mum's condition was dementia, but she understandably and bravely didn't want to provoke anxiety and despair in the family with such a thought, and had kept it to herself. Indeed, one of my company director colleagues had asked me some time earlier if I thought her condition might be frontotemporal dementia as his late mother-in-law had exhibited the same behavioural traits as Vicky in her social disinhibitions – breaking into running when out on walks with people, trying to embrace everyone and lift them off their feet like children – but I always ruled out the possibility of dementia. It was too terrible and definitive to admit there could be no possibility of restoration and recovery for my wife and her generous, loving and giving nature. She was too young, fit and vibrant to admit such a possibility at such an early age. The loss had been too great for me to consider. I was in the 'loss aversion' mode so well described by Daniel Kahneman (see Chapter Four).

I was also thankful that Vicky's FTD was, in the curiously inappropriate way the medical world expresses these things, 'gentle' and not 'aggressive'. Although the prognosis held no hope of recovery, I had found a strange new freedom in having some certainty. I no longer had the dreadful uncertainty of not knowing what was happening. Now it had a name. Now I knew the journey ahead would be long and painful, and it was one of management of Vicky's condition and circumstances, and not of recovery. I didn't know how long the journey would last. It was not remotely what I wanted, it was immensely painful to accept, but it was what we had. They were the brutal facts I could not change.

Imagine you've been suffering abdominal pain for a few days, to the point where you're hoping it's trapped wind but fearing it is cancer. You go to the doctor, and you get the diagnosis and the treatment plan. Now you know what you are dealing with. If it was trapped wind after all (and I've been there and now understand the pain babies experience so much better!), you feel relieved (I thought about avoiding the pun but decided not to just for laughs). If it is cancer, it's devastating but now you know what it is and there may be a good chance of treatment if it has been diagnosed early enough. It's the same with our mental and psychological well-being. Naming the condition meant I knew something of what we were dealing with, even if I didn't want it or know all I wanted to know.

This seemingly perverse sense of finding a new freedom through naming the diagnosis was far from immediate. I can recognise it with hindsight, but it took me several months to get over the initial shock.

The thing I found most helpful to be able to turn the page was accepting the offer of support from a clinical psychologist. I was the classic bloke who never needed help. I didn't think people who needed psychological support were weak or inadequate. I just thought it was for them and not for me. Don't forget, I thought I was indestructible. I had accepted an appointment with a clinical psychologist for both Vicky and me, as I thought it was to help Vicky come to terms with her condition. It was about five minutes before I clocked the appointment was really for me, at which point I went into 'really appreciate the offer but I'm OK' mode.

Have you ever noticed how we see things in other people we don't see in ourselves? Our blind spots? I could see as clear as day Vicky's denial of need for support and help, but I couldn't see my own. The psychologist completed the session with an offer to see me by myself if I ever felt the need. Please credit me with the recognition that I thought that might be possible and at least I kept the door open for the future. And of course, the future arrived as she expected it would.

The downside of naming Vicky's condition was the inescapable burden of responsibility I now felt I had to carry for my life partner. As one of life's natural planners, I was always thinking about tomorrow rather than living in the today. And yet as the months passed by, I noticed I had done very little if anything to plan for the journey we were on. I had no route map. I had avoided researching deeply the subject of FTD, what symptoms to expect and when, how to deal with them, not searching for care packages or care homes or anything else regarding Vicky's future care. And the planners among you will know just how disconcerting and completely against our natures that can be. After all, we want to exert all the control we can over the future by planning for it, don't we?

Out of control

Feeling in control of our lives is a big deal when it comes to our mental well-being. If we see the world as an unfavourable place, we are more likely to try to control it. If we see it as a favourable place, we are more likely to adapt ourselves to it and accept 'it is what it is'. In reality, our only real control is over how we think about what we experience. I'll return to the subject of managing our thoughts in Chapter Thirteen and how we see what we see, but I want to introduce the idea here because it is so fundamental to overcoming grief and finding new meaning in life.

Despite this bizarre new freedom from knowing the diagnosis, I felt utterly out of control. My emotions were all over the place. I had lost my life partner even though she was alive, physically present, strong and fit. To the outside world she was still a friendly woman who was just a bit eccentric and socially embarrassing in her behaviour. I still loved her but now had to live life less as her husband and more as her carer. It was the start of my own change of identity. And that was a big deal. Our daughters had lost the mother who had nurtured them and loved them, even though she was still there physically. They had to shift into parenting mode too in their relationship with her, and into caring mode regarding their concerns for me.

I finally took up the offer of seeing the clinical psychologist again. I explained I had come because I had noticed that I was avoiding researching or preparing for our future. I knew enough to understand that a death from dementia was likely to be painfully slow and gradual, but I didn't know what symptoms might show up along the way, how long it might take, what to do and when to expect what, and I was finding that disconcerting.

She asked me a simple question: 'Why would you want to know?' And that simple question was the key to a strange new freedom I had never previously experienced. It helped me understand that however much I planned, I was not going to be in control. If I could accept I wasn't in control, all I needed to know was how to live in today and how to respond to Vicky's needs and keep her safe.

Letting go

In hindsight, the best decision I made to help with my own emotional well-being was to let go of the things I simply could not control. Sounds easy, but it was both a painful and necessary step.

What do I mean?

I mean that I had to let go of trying to change her future. I had to accept the path we were on and accept that changing it was completely out of my hands.

I mean I had to let go of my irritation that she was in denial about her condition and had no insight into her own deterioration – which ironically was a great blessing, as it meant she suffered less.

I had to stop trying to get her to think differently. Sam, the medic in the family, had to give me the wake-up call, saying, 'Daddy, she can't help how she is thinking. It's not her fault.'

I had to let go of trying to control how she behaved. It was way beyond my pay grade to determine how she would behave, or how quickly or slowly she would decline.

I had to let go of my embarrassment at those socially awkward moments when she would say intrusive or offensive things to complete strangers, or even try to hug and kiss them.

As well as letting go of any pretext that I might have some control over her condition, I had to let go of her spiritually. I remember at our annual Church Faith Camp three years before she died that we were in a time of deep collective worship but I was distressed at the way I could see her acting out publicly during the worship – I simply had to open my arms to the Father, let go and give her back to God.

Letting go helped me understand that the suffering was mine and ours as a family. We suffered knowing this was not the person we knew and loved. But I honestly don't know whether Vicky was suffering herself once she had lost insight into her condition and her mental capacity was so childlike. I could see in her eyes her distress when she didn't feel safe, but once we understood how to read her emotions, it was relatively easy to find ways to help her feel safe and settle her down.

Once I realised the suffering was mine, it gave me some control over it. It wasn't something separate from me, some alien thing that controlled me. It was in my gift to change how I saw and experienced it. I couldn't control it for anyone else, but I could control it for myself.

While it may seem contradictory, it meant that letting go had given me more control and not less.

It's one of those weird things, where the circumstances of life feel out of our control, and the reality is that they were never in our control in the first place. Letting go of any false pretence of controlling what was happening to Vicky, or planning for what should happen next, was a release from the self-imposed stress caused by thinking I *should* be in control, that I should be *doing* something.

Letting go of the pretence of control in no way meant that I gave up responsibility for Vicky's care. That still sat squarely with me and I would not have had it any other way. I was not losing control. I just never had it in the first place. Letting go of control and abdication of responsibility are two entirely different things that easily get confused in how we see life both for ourselves and in others.

I was responsible for Vicky's care, and that meant I was responsible for decisions about her care. As a practical example, when it came to the point where I could no longer care for her safely at home, I was responsible for the choice of care home that could meet her needs. I couldn't control whether specific care homes would accept responsibility for her – and it genuinely knocked me back to find some decided they couldn't take that responsibility after assessing her – but I did have some control over what I would accept on her behalf as a permanent placement. After all, this would likely be her new home for the rest of her life. And in that aspect, I had to persevere and not accept as permanent the two urgent placements that Social Services were able to find when things became unsafe at home.

Understanding I could control how I thought about stuff, and how I exercised my duty of care to my wife, but could control little else, gave me a sense of freedom I had not previously experienced in the journey with Vicky. It didn't reduce my sorrow or grief, but it released me from a burden and extra helping of stress that I didn't need.

Time to reflect

It's that time again to pause and reflect. Please be honest with yourself.

- Have you ever felt out of control only to realise you weren't in control in the first place?
- How might you handle a situation where a loved one is in denial of the danger to themselves and to others?
- When faced with the choice, would you opt for preserving your loved one's safety or their freedom and quality of their life?
- Have you ever carried guilt for something you could not have changed even if you had taken action?

Chapter Nine: A New Reality

Vicky's behaviour over the previous years sadly meant she had become socially isolated at home. While always loving and affectionate, she had started to frighten and even offend people with some bizarre interactions. For example, she would stop people in the street and say inappropriate things, or she would comment on the shape of someone's nose. I knew she was simply trying to connect with people – but just try telling that to an angry stranger in a high street café or the passenger of a car asking for directions, when they are about to explode with indignation. She never became aggressive either verbally or physically, which I know to be the distressing experience of many carers and family of people living with dementia. She remained affectionate and caring to the very last. But there is nothing remotely 'gentle' in watching your loved ones diminish and lose their ability to function as independent human beings. Gradual, perhaps, but never remotely gentle.

One of the consequences of having no language or training to deal with loss through bereavement is that we also lack the skills and knowledge to navigate our way practically through the quagmire of *stuff* that suddenly drops on us. If there was an upside to my experience, it was that letting go of control meant I could start to think properly about planning for the long and tortuous journey that lay ahead. Now my inner planner was finally free to operate within realistic boundaries, knowing there were a small number of things I could control but many more where my only control was over how I thought and acted in the circumstances facing us in the moment.

The diagnosis and realisation that we were now set on an irreversible journey of loss for an indeterminate period meant that even though I had let go of any false sense of control over Vicky's condition, I could not bury my head in the sand and trust to fate a series of practical implications I had so far avoided.

Autonomy and personal care

When she was well, Vicky had made it clear to all of us that she didn't want to be cared for or nursed at home. She hated the idea of losing her personal dignity and the idea of being a burden to her family. Regardless of her condition, however, her sense of personal autonomy was critical to her sense of well-being. What do I mean by autonomy?

Autonomy is an ages-old concept in philosophy and is fundamentally a person's capacity to make an informed decision about their own lives without coercion. At a very stark and simplistic level, it is the difference between freedom to choose and an obligation to obey. In light of the journey with Vicky, I now think of autonomy as something that is fluid over our lifetimes, rather than absolute, and something that is 'felt' or sensed by the person in question. My sense of autonomy is how I feel and act within the boundaries and rules of a more or less free society. Two people can experience the same circumstances and have the same 'legal' freedoms and human rights within the same system of society, and yet they can experience life very differently if one sees the world as an attractive place to engage with and explore, while the other sees life as a threatening and unfavourable place to control.

More to the point for Vicky's story is that her capacity to exercise personal autonomy in a safe way had diminished, objectively speaking, as she regressed in her condition. In simple terms, she was no longer able to do things for herself that she used to be able to do independently. And yet her sense of autonomy seemed to remain intact. How could that be possible?

I found it helpful to think of a child's experience of their autonomy. As a parent and grandparent, I've observed that the parent sets the boundaries for a child's safety: whether those boundaries are high or low risk, the child generally seems to experience pleasure, thrill and adventure when they push or cross the boundaries. By safety, I mean both physical and psychological. If they come out unscathed or unpunished, they push it a bit further until the parent calls a hard stop at a new boundary (and hopes and prays it holds for a while). It seems to me the child's sense of personal autonomy is about their subjective experience, and whether they feel safe or unsafe to act within the boundaries established for them.

Now reverse the flow. With Vicky, it felt like her regression gradually shifted everything in the opposite direction to a child's development. What felt safe to her one day could feel unsafe the next. The reality was heart-rending for her family and loved ones, and meant we had to adjust the boundaries around her so she continued to feel safe.

I will weave some examples into the story that may help carers and families to know what kinds of things to anticipate and how to respond to them. They will invariably be different for differing circumstances, but I hope it will be of some practical help for anyone facing similar situations.

Well before her diagnosis in December 2015, and with hindsight, one of the most marked symptoms of her condition, was her inability to make choices for herself. I will give an example to illustrate the kinds of behaviours to watch out for in suspecting frontotemporal dementia.

In 2011, four years before her diagnosis, Vicky was painfully unable to choose her 'mother of the bride' outfit for Sam's wedding, despite having wanted to do so for several months. She wanted to choose but couldn't choose. Sam had said she would help her but in retrospect, I think Vicky didn't understand the offer. In the end she asked me to choose for her.

To illustrate how tricky this stuff gets, I now realise the mistake I made was to ask Hilary, an old friend of Vicky's, to go shopping with her to help her choose. They used to love clothes shopping together some years earlier, and Hilary always helped Vicky make good choices. Then she moved away with her family and they had lost touch with each other. When I next saw Hilary, she gladly offered to help and take Vicky shopping. I knew Hilary was fun to be with, and she enjoyed helping Vicky look good, so I was confident she would get the job done well.

The problem I hadn't spotted was that they hadn't seen each other for a few years and Vicky no longer recognised Hilary, even though she pretended to. Vicky had asked *me* to choose her clothes for her and I had handed the job over to a long-time friend who was sadly now a complete stranger in Vicky's eyes. The result was that she really disliked the outfit even though it was an attractive choice, just a bit dated. That triggered a deep passive-aggressive anger in her, followed by a troubling depression where she felt she was being forced to spend money on things she didn't like by people she didn't know. Her autonomy had been stolen from her and she must have felt her choices were ignored. Or so it seemed.

To complicate the picture even further, I had a conversation with Hilary about the whole episode the year after Vicky died. She remembered it well and told me how strange she felt it was at the time, because it was Vicky who had chosen the outfit and Hilary had tried to stop her because it was 'too 1980s'. Hilary felt it was too dated and tried to persuade her to buy something more modern and suited to Vicky's style, but Vicky had been adamant about what she wanted. It was only when Hilary told me her account of the episode that I wondered if Vicky had gone back to a dress style that she would have considered stylish in her thirties, associating with the age she had regressed to: still a mature and attractive woman, but who had now travelled back in time to an earlier stage of life. Although she never said it, I now imagine Vicky must have felt threatened being with a stranger who was getting her to spend her money, and more than likely angry with me for not giving her the help she had requested *from me*. It must have been like I had given her autonomy away without her consent.

It's worth noting here this was four years before her diagnosis and nine years before her death. Yes, it's that long a journey. I didn't spot the reasons at the time because I didn't understand what Vicky was going through. I tried to help her change her thinking and how she felt through reasoning, because I believed she had a choice in how she thought and behaved. I clearly failed, but I recount the episode here to help you understand that people with dementia may simply not have a choice in how they think and behave if the wiring in that part of the brain is dying or has already died.

We continued to try to encourage her to make her own decisions, for her to realise she had the freedom and ability to make good choices, but her habit grew of insisting other people make choices for her. The real wake-up call happened for me in a restaurant (First World middle-class problem, I know) when we were with our daughter Rachael. Vicky wanted us to choose her meal for her and we had tried to encourage her to make her own choices instead, pointing out to her the things she normally liked or disliked. In the end, Vicky turned to the embarrassed waitress and insisted she should choose her meal because we would not help her.

The restaurant event was the point when it became clear that she had lost the capacity to choose for herself. She could choose to give the choice to someone she trusted (including a friendly young waitress she had never met before, but who had a lovely smile and patient demeanour) or to me or to Rachael, but she must have hated it being taken away from her without her consent. Therein lay the tricky balance between meeting her need for personal autonomy and understanding what made her feel safe. All of which was compounded by the reality that the boundaries were changing as her regression continued.

As her condition progressed, and even as her insight and self-awareness diminished, she continued to resist fiercely anyone trying to help with her personal care. This included things like applying make-up, where her efforts became increasingly childlike and disinhibited, as well as personal care and dress sense. The physically strong and fit Vicky who was sound in mind guarded her personal independence and autonomy fiercely – and so did the physically strong and fit Vicky with diminished insight and mental capability when it came to her personal care. Her mental fragility was not remotely matched by any physical fragility.

This point about the asymmetry between her mental capacity and physical strength is important because it is far from unique. There are many carers whose partners may be declining mentally yet remain physically strong in ways that make them extremely difficult to manage and keep safe. That is a highly vulnerable position for a carer in terms of their own physical protection and well-being. Policymakers and resource distributors please take note.

Maintaining Vicky's autonomy, independence and dignity for as long as possible was my principal goal. She would have resented and resisted any attempt on my part to control her or restrain her. I don't say this to big myself up, but I say it because I knew she was resourceful and would find ways of getting and doing what she wanted. But I also had to look after myself and sustain as much of my own autonomy as possible for my physical and mental well-being.

What I could do was try to create the conditions for her to be as safe as possible while living as complete and independent a life as possible. I could have taken away her keys, but it wouldn't have stopped her leaving the house. She wouldn't wear an alarm, so I bought her a GPS watch that looked like a piece of jewellery she would choose to wear. I wanted her to have as fulfilling a life as possible while she could, and that meant taking some risks. I just had to find ways to ensure she never went out alone and to learn techniques to let people know Vicky didn't mean to invade their space or offend them, but it was her way of showing them love and engaging with them. To other people that might seem I was taking unnecessary risks, but in my estimation I would rather she lived the remainder of her life as well and enjoyably as possible.

Through her eyes

I could also try to see life through her eyes. Despite the fully grown adult in front of me, I had to understand she was increasingly seeing the world through a child's eyes. Sometimes the world was mysterious, marvellous and full of wonder. And sometimes it was threatening, dangerous, distressing and unsafe.

As her condition progressed, her behaviour became evermore disinhibited in social settings. She would try to hug complete strangers and download to them her thoughts on the limited number of obsessions she carried in her mind. It took me some considerable time to realise that the problem was more about me and my embarrassment than it was about the reaction of some strangers who would only ever experience her for a few brief minutes in their lives. It was her way of showing them love, and so I had to step out of my embarrassment and find little devices to ensure strangers were neither offended by what she said or did, that they understood she was unwell, and that they were able to move on without feeling guilty or rude for disengaging with us.

As she lost her language and the ability to articulate what she was feeling, the only way I knew how she felt was by the look in her eyes. Some of her behaviours became ever more childlike. Like stepping carefully around every flower in a field full of daisies and wildflowers so as not to tread on and 'kill' them. Or helping worms get from one side of a path to another. Or spending hours rescuing flies and insects from outdoor swimming pools. Or stopping to count the horses, birds or sheep in a field when we were out walking. There was little point trying to reason with her and she would be distressed if she could not complete these childlike missions. They gave her pleasure and in her eyes these things were important. That meant it was important for me not to become impatient or try to stop her.

Finding routines and rhythms

As Vicky regressed, I noticed she became more and more reliant on basic routines and habits that were either daily or weekly. She would get anxious and unsettled if she was thrown out of routine, some of which were life-long while others were acquired more recently, so the routines had to be preserved as much as possible. Some frankly verged on the unsafe – like boiling a kettle to fill her hot-water bottle, which she did every night in the latter years whatever the weather, summer as well as winter. Yet even though her mental capacity declined, and she had no insight into the danger of spilling boiling water over herself as she poured it into the narrow hole at the top of the hot-water bottle, she maintained her dexterity very well until the last year of her life.

You might well think I should not have been allowing her to fill a hot-water bottle with scalding water, or doing it for her, but for her well-being I thought I had to support these ways of her exercising some autonomy in helping herself, but staying alert to her changes. In all probability, such was her determination that if I had tried to stop her, she would have done it at another time of day when I wasn't there. Rightly or wrongly, my estimation was that removing her hot-water bottle altogether would simply have caused her more distress than a burn. I figured we could treat a burn, but treating her mental anguish would have been far harder.

Some of her routines, like doing the laundry, went from being twice weekly to daily, regardless of whether there were only a couple items of clothing to wash. I learned to watch this closely for the sake of the planet as well as the household bills as she started to put everything on the hottest maximum wash for over three hours, followed by a two-hour tumble dry every day. I learned a great deal about changing washing machine programmes mid-wash while she wasn't present!

As I have said earlier, I don't use these illustrations to diminish Vicky in any way. I could quote other examples, but my purpose here is to emphasise how important it is for families and carers to look for the subtle but gradual changes in the behaviours *within* the routines as the person's capacity to perform the routine is diminishing even though they remember to keep the routine.

Keeping her safe

My way of managing the risk that she might leave the house alone, and still maintaining her basic freedom, meant I had to detect the consistent patterns and activities in her day and ensure she was safe in those activities.

As the years have passed, I can see how the patterns in Vicky's days had changed in ways I wished I had understood earlier, but that understanding only grew with time. I might have made different decisions if I had known, but the reality is that I couldn't have known, and no one could have told me.

All our journeys are different. Because of that I didn't dwell on what might have been if I had made different choices, and I knew there was no point in blaming myself or feeling guilty, as that was not going to achieve anything positive for either Vicky or me. This may sound cavalier to some, but I say it because I have heard so many stories of carers taking on themselves unnecessary and painful guilt, asking themselves the 'What if I had only …?' questions that have no possible answers when events cannot be re-lived or changed. Guilt-ridden questions about our past choices don't change the nature of the loss carers and family are experiencing. They just compound how we see ourselves failing as carers rather than doing our very best for those we love, however imperfectly we do it. And that does no one any favours.

I found that keeping Vicky safe *and* as independent as possible was a daily balancing act. Her condition was progressive, and her language was gradually diminishing. I kept having to look for new patterns of behaviour or language that told me she had reached a new tipping point in the journey, because she had no way of telling me or expressing what she had lost. I described earlier the image of Vicky's mental faculties as like a Christmas tree whose lights would flicker and eventually die. I had to watch for those kinds of patterns or signals on a daily basis, and check whether other people were seeing them too.

Vicky's daily walks with our dogs provide a concrete example of how her routines became ever more important as her condition progressed. We had always had dogs in the family, and Vicky had always enjoyed taking them out for an hour or so and meeting people on her walks as part of her daily routine. I would always join her when I could. It became obvious in time, however, that walking the dog was more than a way of relaxing and exercising – it had become a necessity around which her day revolved.

There were some loud signals and some very subtle ones. There were some gradual and almost indiscernible declines. And there were some quite dramatic ones too, as evidenced by the next story.

One of the loudest signals came just a few weeks after her diagnosis. Vicky had seemed perfectly capable of walking the dog safely by herself. I would go with her when my work allowed (as previously mentioned, I was working from home). Whenever we walked together, I would watch for her sense of road safety and how she managed our dog, Kaci, on the lead. This may seem a small point, but she had always held the lead when we walked our dogs, and I didn't want to take anything away from her sense of autonomy unless it was absolutely necessary for her safety or for the dog's safety.

One day in the early spring of 2016, Vicky went out with Kaci by herself and didn't return home for a couple of hours. That wasn't unusual as she loved the long walks on the Downs where we live, and would love to stop and chat with people. On this occasion, however, she returned home and when she came upstairs to my office, I could see she was clearly distraught. There were bruises and abrasions on her forehead and face and she pulled up the legs of her jeans to show me more cuts. Her language was very excitable, and she could only tell me she was hurting. I asked her what had happened, and she was unable to tell me. It subsequently took me three days to work out what had occurred from her excitable and piecemeal description of events.

At one point she told me she had been running and went over the top of a car. Later she told me she had died and come back to life. On another occasion, she told me a man brought Kaci back to her and another man was with her when she woke up. As the clues emerged, I realised that she had collided with a car just 50 metres away from our home and only a minute after she had left the house. She must have been running on the pavement with the dog as soon as she left the driveway and ran into a car that was coming out of a neighbouring property. She had lost consciousness for several minutes (which was what she must have meant when she said she had died). I pieced together from her story that she was tended by at least two gentlemen who tried to help her, and someone who brought the dog back. Knowing how independent she was, my guess is that she declined any help when she regained consciousness, and just got up and carried on walking the dog for the next two hours on a long walk up on the South Downs, despite bleeding from the abrasions and the bruising to her face and head.

I read between the lines that the people who had tried to help her would have asked her name and where she lived and tried to get her help. I can only guess that she had now reached the point in her decline where sadly she no longer understood what anyone was saying to her, and she didn't know her own address or name to be able to tell them, as well as any understanding of the danger of running with a dog on a main road. I assume that they would have called for an ambulance, but she recovered before it arrived and insisted on continuing her walk.

That was the tipping point when I knew she was no longer safe to be alone outside the house. That aspect of her independence had now clearly come to a close: it was a risk taken but now a risk too far, and either I had to go with her in future or plan for someone else to be with her and ensure she wasn't alone on her walks.

Once we had established the new routine of always walking together, her first question of the day soon became: 'When are we walking Kaci?' At first, she would be happy with an answer that gave her a time, whether in the morning or the afternoon, and she would then plan her day's other activities around that, especially when she could spend her time painting.

Over time, however, she would become restless and unsettled until she had been out walking, and only settle in her basement studio to paint after walking. Once she was painting, I could be assured she was safe at home and wouldn't go anywhere or do anything else other than come upstairs for meals or make herself a cold drink. Her patterns of daily activity had gradually become very fixed and inflexible, doubtless reflecting a need for safety and assurance through daily repeating patterns in a world where her ability to make choices and act flexibly were gradually diminishing.

I asked a friend who ran a care agency for advice on how to manage from this point onwards. We knew Vicky would find it difficult to have complete strangers in the house to look after her, however professional they might be. She suggested setting up a WhatsApp group of friends and family who knew Vicky and would be willing to help when I was unable to be at home. We put together a group of a dozen or so ladies from family and church friends who would help if they were available. We called the group 'Love Vicky', and they proved a real lifeline for me up until her death, and gave me assurance that the people accompanying Vicky either on her walks or in the house were her friends and knew her history, habits, likes and dislikes. And I know for some of them it gave them an opportunity to show love to both her and to me in a situation where they would otherwise have felt helpless.

In the event, we were able to care for Vicky at home with the help of this dedicated group of family and friends for more than three and a half years after her diagnosis, up until the point where it was unsafe both for her and for me to look after her at home and the time had arrived for admission to a specialist care home.

Leaving home

One of the things that happens when you are in the middle of a loved one's decline and loss of capacity is that your daily reality becomes 'normal', you lose perspective, and you cope and adjust to the next slice of reality. I will be forever grateful to my sister-in-law Lotty for one day taking me aside and saying, 'Enough is enough. You've done all you can and it's time for you to find a care home for her.' I couldn't have reached that point myself without her help, and she gave me the permission I needed to start searching for somewhere that would be acceptable and suitable as Vicky's new home, almost inevitably for the rest of her life.

I started the search with my family and, to my dismay, encountered obstacle after obstacle, mainly because Vicky was under sixty-five and physically stronger and more demanding than the average care home resident with dementia. The one dementia care home I thought would be suitable for her (the one that eventually accepted her) had a long waiting list, as I mentioned earlier, but it turned out not to be possible to wait that long.

Without going into detail, it had become a matter of urgency for her safety, and mine too, that she be admitted to professional residential care. I found her one morning, as one of the milder examples, with burns and blisters on one of her legs that must have been from boiling water – yet she wasn't complaining of pain or even noticing what she had done. She seemed to have lost sensitivity to physical pain. On another occasion, I came down to a kitchen full of gas fumes from an unlit hob on the cooker. Vicky meanwhile was happily washing dishes at the sink and not smelling a thing. Her senses were now depleted to the point that she was a danger to herself and to me. It was clear that we had to act urgently.

Our local Social Services sprang into action and searched for emergency placements, eventually finding a temporary respite placement for two weeks to buy some time until we could find somewhere more permanent.

Other than the day of her death, I can safely say the day of taking her to this first care home was the worst of my life to that point. We could not prepare Vicky, as she didn't understand anything we told her. I felt I was betraying her, packing her bags and some precious belongings, family photographs and an album, her paints, pencils and art materials so she could at least enjoy painting and colouring. Yet I knew she would never return to her home of the previous twenty-seven years, and I felt completely helpless to avoid it.

Rachael came with me to help take and settle Vicky. I was so thankful not to be alone. The home had twenty residents and Vicky was by far the youngest. They had three staff on duty. The inevitable point came when we had to leave and she tried to pursue us down the corridor and had to be restrained by two members of staff. I turned to wave goodbye and the image is engraved in my memory of the sheer panic in her eyes as she struggled to get free and run after us. She couldn't cry out or shout, as her language had gone, but made an anguished piercing sound like a child in distress but unable to speak. I don't tell this story to demean Vicky in any way, or indulge in a pity party. I tell it because this is the kind of horrible reality carers and family have to face with dementia and ultimately, with death.

The care home staff asked me to stay away for a few days to allow Vicky to settle in her new environment. Within twenty-four hours they called me to go in as she would not settle, was constantly trying to escape, testing the doors and trying to open windows, and needed two staff to look after her, to the detriment of the other residents. When I got there, she didn't recognise me – the trauma of her admission to the home had affected her so deeply that she no longer knew who I was, with not even the remotest glimpse of recognition in her eyes as she walked past me to try to open the front door I had just entered. I can only describe her as like a caged bird struggling to fly to freedom. And the care home was clearly not able to provide the supervision she needed to keep her secure or occupied. She managed to escape the home twice in consecutive days. The first time she breached the security with another resident but they were spotted by staff and brought back immediately. On the second occasion, the care home rang me to say she had been found by a local resident one evening wandering the streets and had been brought back by the police, who had contacted the care home to see if they had any residents missing. They didn't know she had gone or how she got out. I don't share this to shame the care home – they were doing the best they could with three staff for twenty highly dependent residents. That was the challenging reality of social care in England in 2019. I pray it will have changed by the time you read this.

Meantime, we continued the search for a more permanent and suitable home, but this time we didn't encounter waiting lists as much as refusals to take her after assessments by different home owners. And while it may be difficult to believe, one of the more expensive private company dementia care homes with nearly sixty residents refused her on the grounds of her disruptive 'moaning'. They clearly could only see the disruption she might cause without understanding she had no other way of communicating the helpless captivity she was feeling.

You just have to laugh

I know this sounds a bit 'off', but while Vicky was compliant with her family and carers throughout most of the journey – and thank goodness she never became angry or violent in the way many dementia cases go – we often had to laugh at the ways she would outwardly comply and then, at her defiant and ingenious best, would attempt to do what she really wanted in the first place.

At first, there were innocent things when she was at home, like blaming the dog for making her do something she said she didn't want to do. Or stuffing her pockets with chocolate biscuits so no one could see how many she had taken from the biscuit barrel. There were more serious things like disguising the fact that she wasn't taking her medications, or only taking the ones she thought she needed. And then there were more dangerous things, like sitting and observing the security measures and the comings and goings of staff in the care home so she could seize her moment to escape when no one was watching. She succeeded via the kitchen when the staff were busy serving food to the residents. On another occasion, the place that became her final home had a spacious and securely fenced garden. Vicky, however, found an eighteen-inch gap between the high railings and a wall that was hidden from sight behind the perimeter bushes.

As she was already known as a 'flight risk', the care home manager had the wisdom to keep watch over her first solo venture into the garden from a distance and saw her find the breach in the fence. The following day he thanked me that she had helped him spot the single weakness in their security so they could close it up. When we heard about this latest attempt to escape, her sister Lotty and I could do nothing other than laugh at her continuing determination and ingenuity to do what she wanted despite her appearance of sweet compliance. Remember I told you earlier that you can't judge a book by looking at the cover?

Time to reflect

Please pause to consider a few more questions before you move on to the next chapter.

- What do you think life looks like through the eyes of a person with dementia or any other terminal or mental condition?
- Would you have removed the hot-water bottle?
- Where would you draw the line on a loved one's autonomy?

Chapter Ten: Taking Care of the Practical and Legal Stuff

Quite aside from the emotional turmoil and bewilderment caused by grief, losing my wife to dementia and subsequently to death, I encountered a labyrinth of legal and practical stuff that created another level of bewilderment, but nonetheless had to be addressed. It was all new to me and I had to learn quickly.

The reality we faced after the diagnosis of dementia was that Vicky had lost mental capacity and would likely need professional care for an indeterminate period of time. I had heard all the horror stories of people having to sell their houses to pay for the care of their loved ones. I knew that Vicky was financially vulnerable and open to abuse, and yet I had no control over her assets because we had not put in place Powers of Attorney over each other's lives. As a result, I was obliged to apply to the Court of Protection for a Deputyship Order to protect her interests. We at least had our wills in place, but they were more than twenty years old.

I knew by reputation that the NHS provided little practical support for the long-term care of people with dementia, but I had no idea just how complex the health and care system was in relation to people with dementia. I knew that any support for her care from local authority Social Services would be means-tested. But I knew little about the legal principles and processes involved, despite my years of working in and around the NHS.

I decided to consult a solicitor when it became obvious that the only way I could get some control over Vicky's assets, in order to protect them, was through the Court of Protection. That sounded really daunting for a newbie to that kind of requirement. I had been to one set of solicitors who quoted an outlandish figure to do the job for me, and then a friend recommended a solicitor who specialised in long-term care. I went to see him to sort out an application to the Court of Protection, and came out of the consultation knowing I could make the application myself and only needed a solicitor for a very limited and specific purpose in the application – all the documents necessary were available online for me to complete.[55] I also came out with an unexpectedly long list of other stuff I really needed to do as speedily as possible to protect my own assets as well as Vicky's. These included revising my will, reviewing the ownership deeds of our house, taking out an LPA over my own life, and – wait for it – intentionally running down Vicky's financial assets as quickly and legitimately as I could once I had control over them. I know the last sentence sounds counterintuitive if my aim was to protect her assets – and it did to me when he first told me. Yet the impeccable reasoning behind his advice will become clear as the story unfolds.

I am going to start with the health and care system, exploring our legal rights in the UK along the way, because the legal stuff opens a better understanding of how the financial stuff works, particularly who pays for what. I am not expert in these subjects, and I cannot overstate the importance of getting good legal advice. You will need to seek professional advice on many aspects of what I describe to be able to determine what is right for you and your loved ones if you are faced with similar circumstances. For that reason, I will stay reasonably light on detail, because every situation is different and my experience will doubtless vary from yours. I will, however, raise the kind of questions you need to face and be prepared for. It also needs a watermark on every page saying *Caveat – please seek professional advice on these matters.*

I will cover briefly in each case:

Navigating the health and care system

- Allowances to support independent living at home
- The legal duties of the NHS
- The legal duties of local authorities for social care

---

55 www.gov.uk/courts-tribunals/court-of-protection (accessed 1.12.23).

Navigating the personal legal stuff

- Do Not Resuscitate (DNR) orders
- Lasting Power of Attorney (LPA)
- The protection of our joint and separate assets
- Court of Protection and Office of the Public Guardian
- The importance of clear wills
- A last word on wills

Navigating the English health and care system

Allowances to support independent living at home

Let's start with the financial support that is available to help people to continue to live independently at home. I will outline later the role of the Office of the Public Guardian (OPG) in the supervision of Vicky's assets after the diagnosis of dementia had been made. The reason to mention them here is that it was through my first contact with the OPG that I discovered the allowances and entitlements that could be claimed on Vicky's behalf to enable her to live independently at home with dementia.

You might think simple logic dictates that financial support or advice for independent living at home with dementia would be administered either through the NHS or Local Government as the two bodies responsible for health and social care in England. You would be wrong. In the first twist of our labyrinthine government public service systems the OPG advised me to apply to the Department of Work and Pensions as the body responsible for the provision of an allowance called Personal Independence Payments (PIPs). The PIP is a really helpful weekly allowance designed to support people to live independently at home where their health condition or disability affects how they can carry out everyday activities and do them safely.

I was very thankful for this support, but only became aware of the allowance nearly two years after Vicky's diagnosis of dementia. I was not advised of its existence through the NHS and yet it is an important element of the public service support I wish I had known about much earlier. The award was backdated to the date of my application, but not to the date of Vicky's diagnosis.

If you are or anticipate becoming a carer for someone with a condition that inhibits their ability to carry out everyday activities, and you have not been aware previously of the PIP allowance, I would commend you to explore it.

The legal duties of the NHS

It may seem strange to write about this so early in the practical stuff, but please bear with me and you will see how it matters to get this clear first. As an aside, it also serves as a commentary on how our UK government systems reflect deeply our culture and national illiteracy around loss.

How so?

For a bit of context, I worked in the NHS for twenty-seven years. I had been privileged to spend twelve of those years as the chief executive of two NHS trusts in the south of England. And yet, even with my history and knowledge of how the health service operates, I was completely lost in the mysterious labyrinth that connects the nationally funded NHS, funded through Central Government, and the social care services that are provided and funded through Local Government, but perversely are highly dependent on Central Government grants.

NHS funding systems are based around the value of the healing, preservation and extension of life – but frankly, avoid paying proper attention to dignified personal and end-of-life care. I need to emphasise here that I am describing the *funding system* and we must differentiate the funding system from the abundant skill and compassion of professional staff who are passionate about the care of vulnerable patients in the last years of their life. The way the hospice movement in the UK is exclusively provided by the charitable sector is a prime example of the low priority given to end-of-life care in the NHS funding system.

The protracted nature of Vicky's journey with dementia gave me time to discover the intricacies of dealing with dementia in England. I emphasise this relates to England and not the whole of the UK, as while many policies and processes in the NHS in England are similar to those of

Northern Ireland, Scotland and Wales, there are also many that differ. If you live in any of the latter three countries, you will need to check the arrangements there.

If my experience was bewildering despite my career working in the health and care system, how much more difficult it must be for people with few if any resources and knowledge of the system that is there to serve them.

I ran into the Kafkaesque nightmare of a system where NHS funding support for people with dementia is completely separate from the means-tested and financially capped funding support from Local Government. The description as Kafkaesque may seem to you a bit of an exaggeration, but please don't dismiss it yet.

Here's the logic. Dementia can only be certified as a *medical* diagnosis by a fully qualified specialist medical practitioner, a consultant psychiatrist employed by or contracted to the NHS. Let me emphasise – both a fully qualified and specialist *doctor*. A GP, a consultant physician or surgeon, or even a doctor undergoing specialty training in psychiatry may be convinced that someone has dementia. And yet their diagnosis has no standing in law, and their diagnosis cannot open any doors to disability allowances or health and social care support. It usually takes around twelve to fifteen years to educate and train such a consultant psychiatrist, at significant cost to the taxpayer (as well as personal cost through student loans and the like).

To apply to the Court of Protection for supervision of Vicky's assets, I had to provide evidence certified by precisely such a qualified and fully trained medical professional regarding her mental incapacity.

To apply for funding to support Vicky to continue to live at home, I had to apply to the Department of Work and Pensions for the PIP. For this purpose, I also had to provide evidence certified by a qualified and fully trained medical professional.

OK so far? Still with me?

Here's the next point.

The NHS is an admirable system, free at the point of delivery. Right? So you would think according to the Introduction to the NHS Constitution,[56] which says:

---

56 www.gov.uk/government/publications/the-nhs-constitution-for-england/the-nhs-constitution-for-england (accessed 1.12.23).

The NHS belongs to the people.

It is there to improve our health and wellbeing, supporting us to keep mentally and physically well, to get better when we are ill and, when we cannot fully recover, *to stay as well as we can to the end of our lives.* It works at the limits of science – bringing the highest levels of human knowledge and skill to save lives and improve health. *It touches our lives at times of basic human need, when care and compassion are what matter most.*[57]

The NHS Constitution describes seven underpinning values, including:

1. The NHS provides a comprehensive service, available to all

It is available to all irrespective of gender, race, disability, age, sexual orientation, religion, belief, gender reassignment, pregnancy and maternity or marital or civil partnership status. The service is designed to improve, prevent, diagnose and treat both physical and mental health problems with equal regard. It has a duty to each and every individual that it serves and must respect their human rights. At the same time, it has a wider social duty to promote equality through the services it provides and to pay particular attention to groups or sections of society where improvements in health and life expectancy are not keeping pace with the rest of the population.

2. Access to NHS services is based on clinical need, not an individual's ability to pay

NHS services are free of charge, except in limited circumstances sanctioned by Parliament.

With me so far?

Here's the first twist in the labyrinth.

Access to NHS funded support for long-term conditions like dementia, such as long-term nursing home care, is determined by the rules in place for a mechanism called NHS Continuing Healthcare funding (CHC). And

---

57 Emphasis mine.

here's where we suddenly end up back at the beginning of the labyrinth, because NHS CHC funding operates with a separate and limited set of criteria to the rest of NHS treatment and care.

I was mistaken to think that CHC funding was covered by the NHS Constitution pledge of a 'comprehensive service, available to all' designed to 'improve, prevent, diagnose and treat both physical and mental health problems', 'when care and compassion are what matter most'.

I think most reasonable people would consider that someone should fall within the NHS Constitution criteria if:

- They need nursing care in a nursing care home registered to provide specialist dementia care.
- They are there because of a mental health condition.
- The condition was diagnosed by a fully trained and qualified medical professional who was trained at public (and personal) expense for twelve to fifteen years to be able to make the diagnosis.
- The diagnosis was based on the expert medical advice of a specialist neuro-radiologist, also trained at public and personal expense for twelve to fifteen years to be able to give the opinion to the psychiatrist.
- The neuro-radiologist had given their opinion as a result of an expensive MRI scan provided by the NHS in an NHS hospital.

Well, apparently not.

To qualify for CHC funding, it must be proven that you have a 'primary health need', which is an expression created specifically to describe eligibility for NHS Continuing Healthcare funding by the Department of Health.[58] It is a concept that is used as the key criterion for eligibility – it is not a legal definition sanctioned by Parliament. It means that your care requirements

---

58 Page 7, para. 4 of the National Framework for NHS Continuing Healthcare and NHS-funded nursing care' (October 2018) states: 'Primary health need' is 'a concept developed by the Secretary of State to assist in determining when the NHS is responsible for providing for all of the individual's assessed health and associated social care needs.' See www.gov.uk/government/publications/national-framework-for-nhs-continuing-healthcare-and-nhs-funded-nursing-care (accessed 19.12.23).

are primarily for healthcare, rather than social or personal care needs. And here's the next Kafkaesque twist.

Vicky was assessed for her eligibility to NHS CHC funding. She had been diagnosed by a specialist consultant psychiatrist in dementia. The requirement for her to be admitted to a nursing home specialising in dementia care was entirely a result of her medical condition of dementia. Her inability to manage her own life and affairs in any way safely was entirely down to her dementia. The total loss of her ability to lead an independent life was entirely down to her dementia. This was not remotely a matter of someone needing some support to live independently at home because of their age or physical disability.

The decision of the local NHS Continuing Care assessor, confirmed by an NHS Continuing Care panel, was that Vicky's need for care was not, and I quote, because of a 'primary health need'.

Those three seemingly innocent little words are the crux of the issue. By default, they mean that the assessor and the panel considered Vicky's need for admission to a specialist dementia nursing care home to be caused by her social or 'personal care' needs. In other words, the professional opinions of expensively trained and highly specialised consultants in psychiatry and neuro-radiology, which were required as proof for the Court of Protection and the Department of Work and Pensions applications, suddenly counted for nothing with the NHS. The Continuing Healthcare part of the NHS system had decided that her primary need was not a 'health need', and was judged *by a panel of NHS assessors*, to be a matter for social care (and therefore Local Government) and not the NHS.

Do you still think I was exaggerating when I said the system was Kafkaesque?

The eagle-eyed cynics among you might now be thinking that the legal get-out clause in the NHS Constitution that NHS services are free of charge 'except in limited circumstances sanctioned by Parliament' might have been used to make an exception for NHS Continuing Healthcare. You would be wrong. Responsibility for the legal framework for CHC is delegated by Parliament to the Department of Health. The NHS Constitution says: 'NHS services are free of charge, except in limited circumstances sanctioned by Parliament.'[59] In this case the criteria for eligibility for NHS Continuing

59 www.gov.uk/government/publications/the-nhs-constitution-for-england/the-nhs-constitution-for-england (accessed 18.12.23).

Healthcare funding have been introduced by the Department of Health but not directly sanctioned by Parliament as required by the NHS Constitution. Section 56 of the National Framework for NHS Continuing Healthcare and NHS-funded Nursing Care says:

> An individual has a primary health need if, having taken account of all their needs (following completion of the Decision Support Tool), it can be said that the main aspects or majority part of the care they require is focused on addressing and/or preventing health needs. Having a primary health need is not about the reason why an individual requires care or support, nor is it based on their diagnosis; it is about the level and type of their overall actual day-to-day care needs taken in their totality.

As a further complication, local authorities are prohibited by law 'from providing, or arranging for the provision of, nursing care by a registered nurse.'[60] In other words, care by a registered nursing practitioner can only be arranged either privately or by the NHS. So, if someone's day-to-day needs require the supervision of a registered nursing practitioner and local authorities are prohibited by law from providing or arranging such care, and the NHS assessors decide the person requiring care does not meet the eligibility criteria for CHC, the only remaining options are NHS-funded nursing care at a significantly lower rate[61] than CHC funding or private funding[62] or a combination of both.

I will leave the campaigning side of that debate about the lawfulness of NHS Continuing Healthcare funding to fabulous websites like Care

---

60 Section 22(3) of the Care Act 2014 says: 'A local authority may not meet needs under sections 18 to 20 by providing or arranging for the provision of nursing care by a registered nurse'. See https://www.legislation.gov.uk/ukpga/2014/23/section/22/enacted (accessed 19/12/23).

61 £209 per week (source www.nhs.uk/conditions/social-care-and-support-guide/money-work-and-benefits/nhs-funded-nursing-care/) (accessed 14.12.23).

62 People meeting NHS CHC eligibility criteria have their full costs met. Full costs of care will vary geographically. In our area, the weekly rate for a registered dementia nursing home ranged from £1,250 to £1600 per week.

To Be Different.[63] My purpose here has been to tell the story around our practical experience to help others who may have to navigate these dark and choppy waters.

The legal duties of local authorities for social care

It really matters to understand how social care works in England in the kind of circumstances I experienced, because so many people get caught up in the system in unnecessarily distressing ways in the later years of life, either being cared for or as carers.

Given Vicky's condition, I realised we would only be able to care for her for so long through our family and friends network before she needed professional care at home, or possibly specialist residential and nursing care for people living with dementia.

I was aware before visiting the solicitor that access to social care support was financially means-tested: in other words, people only qualify for financial support if they have money or assets below a defined financial threshold.

Bearing in mind my history in the NHS and in subsequent consulting roles for Health and Local Government for several years prior to this consultation with a solicitor, I now realised I didn't have a clue about how it worked in practice. I had managed more or less successfully (probably less) to navigate one labyrinth only then to encounter another, but this time with a big entry fee.

Medical services in the NHS, with the exception of prescription charges,[64] are free at the point of delivery and available to all regardless of economic status.[65] Unlike the NHS, however, social care is not a free service available to everyone regardless of economic status.

Local authorities have always had to charge for care services. This means that service users are sometimes exposed to potentially very high and unpredictable care costs and face a genuine possibility of losing the majority of their income and assets.

---

63 https://caretobedifferent.co.uk (accessed 1.12.23).

64 Please note that medical services in the NHS are separate legally to dental services within the NHS.

65 There are other significant exceptions like dentistry and optometry (eye care).

I knew the threshold to qualify for social care funding support from our local authority was set as £23,500 at the time.[66] I blithely assumed Vicky would not qualify for social care funding support from the local authority because our joint assets were significantly higher than that, especially taking our home into account. I went into the solicitor's office thinking that once our savings were spent on Vicky's care, we might have to sell the house to fund care for the remainder of her life.

I may not be the sharpest knife in the drawer when it comes to understanding the mysterious labyrinth of social care funding, and I fully acknowledge that our financial status was relatively privileged, but it came as a complete surprise to me when the solicitor told me the assessment only applied to the assets of the person needing care and not to the joint assets that included the spouse.

At this point I will leave aside the political arguments about the point at which a local authority should pay for someone's care; my central purpose in this explanation is to offer practical help to those who find themselves in the circumstances that I encountered.

Here's what else was news to me. Vicky's share of our home would not count towards the local authority calculation of her financial assets *because I was living there.* It was news to me because I had heard and read so many stories of people having to sell up their homes to pay for their spouse's care that I assumed it to be the law. It isn't. No married person need sell their home to pay for their spouse's care if it is also their home. At a stroke the qualifying threshold for Vicky to receive state-funded care had suddenly come into reach instead of feeling like it was on another planet. I will not venture here into the tricky world where, for example, a daughter or son lives with a parent as their carer and the parent goes into care. I can only advise the carer to consult a solicitor as early as possible or an organisation such as Age UK or Carers UK, so that they know how best to protect their own rights as well as the assets of the person needing care well before the time arrives when residential care is required.

Leaving the solicitor's office knowing that our home and my assets would be protected was worth his fee already for the peace of mind it gave me.

---

66 It's called the 'capital limit' in the legal social care jargon.

I promised earlier to explain the process to run down Vicky's financial assets as quickly as I legitimately could to get her bank accounts, regular income and savings below the threshold level of £23,500 to qualify for social care funding support. It so happened I received this advice from my solicitor two years before it became necessary to involve Social Services in Vicky's care, and it was perfectly feasible over those two years (and approved by the Office of the Public Guardian) to spend her current account cash and savings on the costs of maintaining her at home. Her personal care items, clothing, her share of the food bills, energy costs, house insurance and a host of other items of expenditure were allowed by the OPG and by Social Services.

The time sadly arrived when it became clear that Vicky wasn't safe being cared for at home because she had lost all insight into the hazards around her while still fully mobile and physically active. And I was at risk too in ways I could not have imagined, manage or mitigate. At that point I turned to Social Services, and they stepped in to arrange urgent respite care for Vicky for a couple of weeks while we searched for a suitable longer-term home. I was grateful for the respite but also devastated emotionally by the presenting reality that Vicky would never return to the house she had made our home so many years earlier.

I will spare you much of the detail of our journey over the next couple of months, but the point I want to make is that our only legal entitlement as citizens to social care in England is to have the situation *assessed* by a social care professional. That's it. There is no entitlement to funded care unless the person needing care has personal assets below the qualifying financial threshold I have described. Imagine the furore it would cause if government proposed that the only support citizens receive from the NHS is to have our conditions and diseases assessed or diagnosed, but access to healthcare treatment was to be means-tested according to our income and assets?

When the time came for the local authority to undertake the financial assessment, I had to provide two years' worth of bank and savings account statements for Vicky to be able to prove that I had not run down her assets fraudulently in anticipation of her needing social care support. In short, I couldn't have beaten the system even if I had tried. Local authorities are very hot on what they consider 'deprivation of assets' in social care, whereby they examine whether someone has removed their assets from the local authority's reach deliberately to avoid paying a contribution by giving assets to someone else.[67] It is described in the 'Care and Support Statutory Guidance' issued under the Care Act 2014, Annex E6) as: 'Deprivation of assets means where a person has intentionally deprived or decreased their overall assets in order to reduce the amount they are charged towards their care.'

Contrary to my expectations, when the time came for her to need professional care, the local authority financial assessment helped identify several additional items that I could legitimately charge against her accounts. They did their best to help her qualify for funded support, in stark contrast to the NHS Continuing Care commissioner who did their best to disqualify her. As a result, she qualified for funded social care support.

The next complication, if a person qualifies for financial support from Social Services, is the weekly limit the local authority will pay for care. Depending on the costs of care in whatever part of the country you live, the weekly limit may or may not be adequate to pay for good quality care in the kinds of environment we would all wish for our loved ones if it is to be their home for the remainder of their lives.

There is in addition the option for a family or carer to supplement, or top up the local authority contribution, but with the catch that the assets of the person needing care *cannot be used* for that purpose and must be provided by a third party. In other words, I was not able to use any of Vicky's financial assets as a contribution to pay for her care.

I was in the fortunate position of being able to pay the top-up fees for Vicky's care without having to sell our home, but I know that is not the case for some carers and families who have to dispose of their financial assets to pay for dignified care for their loved ones.

In summary, we had entered the labyrinth with a diagnosis of dementia certified by a qualified medical professional and exited bewildered by our English health and care system, along with a reduced bank balance and depleted emotional reserves.

---

67 Department of Health, 'Care and Support Statutory Guidance', issued under the Care Act 2014, Annex E6, www.gov.uk/government/publications/care-act-statutory-guidance/ care-and-support-statutory-guidance (accessed 19.12.23).

Navigating the personal legal stuff

My first point here involves the highly emotional dilemma faced by so many carers and families of deciding whether or not a loved one should be resuscitated in the event of a catastrophic health event.

Do Not Resuscitate (DNR) orders

When Vicky went into a care home, we had to face up as a family to the reality that she would most likely die without returning to our home. We all knew that death caused by dementia could at worst be cruel and lingering, and her condition was irreversible.

I had open conversations with all our daughters to find out their wishes if she suffered a collapse or heart attack. The insight of our middle daughter, Sam, a medical doctor, about the processes involved in resuscitation and artificial life support on a hospital ventilator, confirmed for us all that we did not want Vicky's life prolonged unnecessarily if she suffered a catastrophic event. Knowing how distressed she got in unfamiliar settings, we took the decision together to request the care home to establish a DNR order that would allow her to die peacefully when the time came.

It may sound cold and clinical to make such a decision over a loved one, but it was really one of the hardest decisions I have ever had to face in my life. I had heard one too many stories in my career of people being cared for at home who subsequently died in cubicles in hospital emergency departments after transportation by ambulance because there was no DNR order in place to allow the person to die peacefully at home.

Ambulance crews and A&E staff have a duty to save and preserve life wherever possible, but they can be released from the duty to perform cardiopulmonary resuscitation (CPR – restarting the heart), and hence transporting to hospital if there is a DNR order in place.

DNR orders are known technically as advance directives or advance decisions. An advance directive is a legally binding document that states a person's wishes about receiving medical care if they are no longer able to make medical decisions because of a serious illness or injury.[68] Advance directives may also give someone such as a spouse, relative or friend the authority to make medical decisions for another person when that person can no longer make decisions.

I advised the care home that we wished to put in place a DNR order. Signing the document felt emotionally like I was signing Vicky's death warrant – but it was handled with great sensitivity by the matron. In the event I was glad we had the hard family conversation and made the decision well ahead of time.

I have previously mentioned the GP responsible for her care rang me to ask our wishes in case she caught the virus and needed hospital care. The GP's call was providential, as three days after the call, Vicky contracted COVID-19 and died just eleven days later. However deeply painful that was, I was grateful at least that neither the care home staff nor I had to make any on-the-spot decisions, and that she was able to die peacefully in the room that had been her home for the previous eight months.

I would never pretend the decision to establish a DNR order is anything but painful. It means we have to face up to the reality that a loved one will die. I would commend, however, that where there are other family members, no one should take the decision alone and without a conversation and agreement wherever possible. I recognise there may not always be other close family – in which case establishment of an LPA may offer the opportunity to have the loved one in question have their wishes expressed in the eventuality that they might lose physical or mental capacity (see next section). Alternatively, there may be surviving friends who can help make the decision, or the person's GP. The worst of all worlds must be to do it alone and find other family members or close friends believing, after the death, that everything possible should have been done to preserve the life of the loved one with medical intervention. It's just another raw but practical example of why we need to talk about death before it arrives.

---

68 www.nhs.uk/conditions/end-of-life-care/planning-ahead/advance-decision-to-refuse-treatment (accessed 14.12.23).

Lasting Power of Attorney

Vicky had been wise enough to get us to make mirroring wills in our late thirties. I hadn't thought them necessary, but she won the day with the argument that if anything happened to us together, we would want our children never to be separated and also for them to be cared for by named relatives. That in turn meant we had to have explicit conversations with our own siblings about the arrangements we would want for our children, so they were not left to chance or the judgement of the courts. Once the wills were made we paid no attention to them at all. We thought the job was done. In one way it was, but in another way it wasn't.

I now regret that we had not also given each other LPA over each other's affairs for both care of our assets and decisions regarding our healthcare if either of us lost our mental capacity or if anything happened to one of us.

I shared earlier how I discovered she was being financially abused during the early onset of dementia, and yet I could not do a single thing about it as I had no legal power over her affairs. I could not speak to her bank as I had no authority over her account, and we had no LPA in place. In the event I could only apply to the Court of Protection to be approved as her deputy after a medically attested diagnosis of dementia and diminished mental capacity had been provided for Vicky.

There are two types of LPA: one for financial decisions and another for health and care decisions. In our case we had neither. They are relatively easy to establish. The Office of the Public Guardian in the UK provides the necessary forms and information on the process[69] and the LPA must be registered with the OPG before it can be used.

Needless to say, I now have the LPA in place over my own life for both my financial affairs and my health and care needs if the situation arises where I am unable to make the necessary decisions.

The protection of our joint and separate assets

The issue of the joint and separate assets of a married couple was a complete

---

69 www.lastingpowerofattorney.service.gov.uk/home (accessed 18.12.23).

mystery to me before I went through this process. I had always felt that in a loving relationship, talking about the legal protection of our joint and separate assets would feel a bit cold and mercenary. It would be thinking of protecting myself against the breakdown of my marriage and possible divorce, all based on an absence of trust or a failed relationship. My assumption was that the only way our marriage would end would be through one or both of us dying.

Reviewing and changing our home ownership deeds was not on the agenda when I first went to consult the solicitor. But in the sad reality that now faces so many couples when dementia strikes, it was necessary to separate and protect my own assets while still married because Vicky had lost mental capacity through no fault or choice of her own. I now had to face the outside possibility that I might die before her, and my assets would go into trust on her behalf unless I changed my will and additionally severed the joint tenancy of our home.

In practical terms, changing my will was relatively painless. Severing the joint tenancy of our home, however, was deeply painful for me emotionally. Like so many couples, we had always bought our homes in our joint names, not remotely understanding there were two types of joint ownership, those of 'joint tenancy' and 'tenants in common'.

In the joint tenancy situation, the ownership of our home would pass outright to Vicky as my surviving spouse if anything happened to me, in effect into a trust supervised by the Court of Protection.

As tenants in common, Vicky's half share of ownership would pass to her but my half share would pass by will to my heirs and not automatically to the surviving joint owner. That way I knew my children could exercise control over my half share of the house, while stipulating in my revised will that Vicky would have a right of occupation in my share of the house rent-free for as long as she needed.

Court of Protection and Office of the Public Guardian

The process to be Vicky's legally appointed deputy for her financial affairs and assets took both significant time and money to gain approval. It made me accountable to the Court of Protection through the provision of annual accounts for her assets and supervision by the OPG.

By and large, the OPG supervision was a light touch where I could demonstrate clear patterns of historical expenditure. Much depended, however, on the supervising officer, even to the point where one officer told me I had to repay personally several thousand pounds to Vicky's account for financial gifts to our grandchildren that had previously been approved by two of the officer's colleagues. Fortunately, I had kept records of all correspondence of the prior approvals and was eventually able to get the decision overturned.

The obvious learning from this is both to keep good records of all correspondence with official bodies and keep them in order, as you never know if or when they will be required. The less obvious lesson is not to expect consistency of treatment necessarily between one official and another from the same organisation regarding the same issue. Sad but true. And before anyone from the OPG who happens to be reading takes offence about inconsistency of decision-making, the reality is that you are in the very good company of judges, doctors, loss adjustors, insurers and many other professionals. Please read *Noise* by the Nobel Prize-winning behavioural economist Daniel Kahneman and eminent colleagues if you need convincing.[70]

I appreciate completely the need for the Court of Protection to safeguard the assets of vulnerable people, but the key learning point here is that having Lasting Powers of Attorney over each other's lives would have saved me several months' worth of complex time-consuming work and expense to have to register with the Court of Protection and continuously satisfy the OPG about how I was administering Vicky's assets.

I mentioned earlier there are two types of LPA. One for health and welfare and one for property and financial affairs.

A health and welfare LPA gives your attorney (the nominated person to whom you have given the power) the power to make decisions about your daily routine (washing, dressing, eating), medical care, moving into a care home and life-sustaining medical treatment. It can only be used if you're unable to make your own decisions.

A property and financial affairs LPA gives your attorney the power to make decisions about your money and property. This includes managing your bank or building society accounts, paying bills, collecting your pension

---

70 Daniel Kahneman, Olivier Sibony and Cass Sunstein, *Noise* (London: William Collins, 2021). The authors examine the topic of human error in decision-making, caused by bias and noise or unwarranted variation.

or benefits and, if necessary, selling your home. Once registered with the OPG, it can be used immediately or held in readiness until required.

In retrospect, a combination of the health and welfare LPA and the property and financial affairs LPA would have been the best route to manage Vicky's affairs. But by the time it was needed it was too late to apply, as Vicky's mental capacity to make an informed decision was already severely prejudiced.

Later down the line, when I came to apply for funding support from the NHS for Vicky's care home placement for the last eight months of her life, the fact that I had only applied to the Court of Protection for powers over Vicky's assets and property, and not for her health and welfare, was perversely used as evidence against our application for NHS Continuing Care funding. Yet another perplexing demonstration of the labyrinthine experience I shared earlier about my engagement with the NHS.

The importance of clear wills

The rubber hits the road in relationships when it comes to money, and this is never more true than in the case of inheritances. I have mentioned previously how Vicky had been wise enough, despite my resistance, to have us make mirroring wills in our late thirties.

Neither of us could have anticipated at the time that one of us might lose our mental capacity, which would in turn have made it impossible to draft a will in a way that expressed the individual's intentions when healthy and well. Under the Mental Capacity Act 2005, if someone loses mental capacity their will can be made by application to the Court of Protection as a Statutory Will. The application itself costs several hundred pounds, quite apart from solicitor's fees and counsel's fees in cases of dispute. Easier by far, though not without cost, to make clear and simple wills in the first place when both parties are of sound mind.

The other thing to understand is that once a person is under the supervision of the Court of Protection, their will can only be amended by that same process of a Statutory Will. While I held copies of our wills, I had no power over Vicky's will as her Court of Protection appointed deputy.

Her will was lodged with and held by the originating solicitors subject to probate being granted. I don't mention that as a problem, just a reality to help with expectations.

I cannot overstate the importance of getting good legal advice in this matter.

Quite apart from the practical importance of clear wills there is enormous importance in understanding the emotional impact of one's will on descendants.

The intense period of grief is a painful time following the death of a family member. It is a period when families can fall apart. The division of goods and assets in a will is highly charged emotionally. Newspapers are full of stories over contested wills and provide a sad commentary on the power of the deceased even after death to separate and fragment families. I have also seen in friends how the grief of death can be compounded by shock, disbelief and a sense of injustice at the perceived unfair and unexplained distribution of parents' assets to their children in their wills.

Here again I pay tribute to Vicky's wisdom in telling our children, when she was in good health, what they would each receive, as she wanted them to feel fairly treated and loved without favouritism. Her example led me to ensure that the revision of my will after her diagnosis with dementia was fully transparent to our children and felt fair by them all before it was finalised.

A last word on wills

While resolving differences in the living years is so much more than wills alone, the use of a will to express personal judgements and disagreements with family members can be a cruel legacy beyond the grave.

In the vast majority of cases, legacies are straightforward and there is nothing that needs to be hidden during the deceased's lifetime. Where that is the case, I don't see what is to be gained by shrouding the intentions of our wills in mysteries to be revealed by a solicitor when we die. Failing to do so is simply another example of how we avoid talking about death in our culture, when there are actions we can take in life that can lessen the complications and pain caused by our deaths.

Of course, circumstances can change between drawing up a will and our deaths, but those matters can also be discussed in life rather than after our deaths if the will needs revision.

And if you think your will is not going to be straightforward, please don't fall into the trap of leaving things unsaid or unresolved to the extent that is possible. I have seen in friends the devastation and family break-down caused by wills where the legacies were unevenly distributed, but the reasoning behind the distribution was never explained and remained subject to damaging speculation.

Resolution of deep disagreements in the living years can be extremely difficult and not always possible – but why on earth compound the grief caused by death by simply neglecting to name and resolve the pains of life while we still have time? Even where resolution of differences may not be possible, for whatever reason, the choice to forgive wrongs caused in this life while all the parties are still alive is infinitely preferable to forgiveness after death. Leaving it to beyond the grave may feel like the easy way out, but it can also make the pain of our deaths so much harder than necessary for those we leave behind.

Life is unpredictable and we don't get to choose when it will end, or the way it will end. Sometimes it's predictable and drawn out. Sometimes it is shockingly sudden. It will, however, end.

Whichever way it happens will be painful enough for the bereaved to process their grief and pain without the added grief of finding they have been treated unequally in the will for reasons they can only imagine or discover through third-party whispers.

Let's be more literate than that in how we engage with the inevitability of our deaths. Let's have the courage to sort these things out in the living years.

Time to reflect

Time to pause now for some reflection and some questions to get you started:

- Were you aware of the NHS Continuing Healthcare financial arrangements? Please check them out as soon as possible if you think a loved one may need continuing care.

- Do you understand your rights to live in your home if the owner (or joint owner) of the home has to go into care?
- Do you have a will in place that you think is fair to your descendants?

Chapter Eleven: Death and the Point of No Return

Songwriters and poets get this stuff about our everyday lives, loss and our humanity.

Just nine days before Vicky died, Switchfoot released a single called 'Joy Invincible'[71] that captures the devastation of the death of a loved one:

And all the plans we held for the future
And all the memories up from the past
The world I once knew
Was in a cardboard box
In the lobby lost and found

Earlier, I told you about my M27 experience when I broke down weeping in the outside lane of the motorway. It was like I was enveloped in a dream that could have had catastrophic real-life consequences if I hadn't managed to cling on to some sense of reality.

And the same could be said of the day of Vicky's death. That feels like a dream now too, a parallel universe where all reason, logic and meaning in life broke down.

Neither I nor my family had been allowed to see Vicky in the last seven weeks of her life, or get to be with her when she died. I just had the words of a compassionate carer reassuring me that my wife had died peacefully … after it had happened. But that was all.

In those few minutes my world fell apart. I was alone at home. I was

---

71 'Joy Invincible' written by Jon Foreman and Tim Foreman. Copyright © Gangs Of Palomar Publishing; Penny Farthing Music. Administered by Concord Music Publishing. All rights reserved.

utterly desolate. I couldn't go anywhere. I couldn't go and see anyone. And now I had the job of letting all the family know. There was no one else to do it for me.

I was so grateful to our local undertakers where the lady on call that Sunday afternoon just took away all the burden of the practical stuff, like removal of Vicky's body from the care home. Her empathy and understanding of exactly what to do in the extraordinary circumstances of a death from COVID-19, in the middle of a national lockdown, was an immeasurable relief. I could get on with my meltdown and not have to worry about practicalities. I learned those following weeks never to underestimate the value and skills of a good local undertaker in such moments of crisis and grief. Genuine gold-dust in dark times.

That Sunday was the hardest day of my life. Even though I knew Vicky was dying slowly and she had reached a very infant-like state, the reality of her death was something I was never prepared for. It didn't matter how many times I had rehearsed the moment and how I thought I might react, there was no possible preparation for the deep anguish and emotional turmoil I experienced. I was thankful she hadn't died the worst of a death from dementia or the worst of the agonies of death from COVID-19, but the pain was like nothing I had ever experienced in my life. This was the start of my second cycle of grief.

I doubt that learning the language of death, or more conditioning about it earlier in life, would have made a shred of difference to my pain at that point. Ironic, really, when you think that's part of what this book is about. But the reality is there are no words to describe the depth of pain I experienced in those moments and days. I went to bed weeping, and I woke up weeping for days on end. That kind of pain had a language all of its own that I felt deep in my soul, but I cannot remotely articulate with words.

During the pandemic, even funerals were cut down and restricted affairs. For Vicky's funeral we were allowed twelve immediate family members, plus my church pastor. We weren't allowed to hold wakes after the funeral to mourn with friends and wider family. Promise not to tell the authorities, but we bent the rules and gathered in the garden of our home after the funeral to toast Vicky's memory and spend some precious hours together remembering her, loving and consoling one another as best we could. I half-jokingly told everybody I would pay any fines that were issued, but the truth is our need to be together at that time was overwhelming, regardless of any restrictive laws in place.

Intense grief

When Vicky died, I realised I was in intense grief. I thought I knew what grief was following her diagnosis, but I didn't know who or what this new intruder really was, this thing called intense grief. Now that I was on speaking terms with grief, I wanted to know more, so I decided I had to find out. I did a couple of things we can all do.

Firstly, I started to read and learn about the processes and experience of grief. I had asked a couple of friends, one a psychotherapist, the other a counsellor, to recommend some good books. They equipped me with some clarity about what I was experiencing and taught me how unique everyone's experience of grief is. They validated my experience, and I began to understand my frequent meltdowns, my loss of motivation, my rotten patterns of sleep, my lack of focus, my comfort in a glass or several of wine. And so on. But I was still in DIY mode.

Secondly, my eldest daughter, Ali, told me she was enrolling for the Bereavement Journey course[72] and asked if I wanted to join too. It was only one night a week for six weeks and was free of charge. I said I would think about it, but I really didn't want to because I thought I was doing OK with my self-help approach.

Then I had this question for myself: 'What makes you so special that you don't think you need any more help?' In classic man style I had persuaded myself I was 'doing OK', when probably I was afraid of letting strangers into my life and exposing my emotions in front of them, like a helpless and vulnerable child. What I had really been doing was trying to keep my 'indestructible me' and my pride intact. So I took the risk. After all, I reasoned I could withdraw if I wanted and it wasn't going to cost anything.

I did the course and benefited so much that I immediately volunteered to run one in my church, and another one, and then another one and then

---

72 https://thebereavementjourney.org (accessed 1.12.23).

another one. The course helped me see beneath the veneer of respectable normality in our 'civilised' lives, and I saw for the first time in my privileged life the horrible pain of people who, like me, had never been taught to deal with loss and who had no language or preparation for it. It was like I had learned a new language in those few weeks that could help me move through my journey and get myself unstuck in my grief, and maybe even help others too.

The language of loss is really pretty simple. It's not complex at all. For me, it started with trying to understand what was going on in myself and then letting someone in to help me process it, however much it hurt.

The change of identity

When the Registrar of Births and Deaths recorded my status as a widower, I had a violent visceral reaction – it felt like he had stabbed me in the guts. It felt like someone had just changed my identity without my permission.

Within days I received the first of several official letters addressed to me about *the late* Mrs A.N.V. Greene. Vicky was no longer a living person; she was a *late* person. She was no longer my wife. She was my *late* wife. And just in case you are wondering, the A.N.V. stood for Anne Noreen Victoria, but she was always known as Vicky.

Like it or not, the identity I had carried as a husband for forty-one years had changed in the very moment Vicky breathed her last breath. After that last breath, we were no longer Vicky and Roger to our friends and family. We were no longer Mum and Dad to our children. We were no longer Gaggy and Avo to our grandchildren. We were no longer Mr and Mrs Greene to the wider world. I hadn't asked for it and I hadn't expected it. It was just a new identity I would have to get used to.

Identity changes are a big deal. They go to the heart of who we are and how we pitch up in the world.

They can be causes for celebration. A new job, a new qualification, a promotion at work, a new partner, a new baby in the family are all changes in our identity that we may have worked for, ambitions we may have achieved, and we celebrate them, and those around us celebrate with us. We have gained something valuable and we're on the upward journey in life. They are significant and transformational moments in our lives that bring joy, optimism and hope. They are the golden moments when 'life never felt so good'. Life is never what it was and never will be again. We feel like our lives are growing and our horizons are expanding.

The other side of the coin is that loss of any type also brings a change in our identity, who we are and how the world sees us. The loss of my wife was the loss of my life companion, my best friend and confidante, the mother of our children, the loss of our future together. It's a change in identity I never signed up for and would never have chosen for myself.

These changes of identity can be causes for sadness, despair, anger, hopelessness and even denial. Life is never what it was and never will be again. I felt like I was getting smaller, closing in on myself, my horizons and possibilities diminishing. The very idea of growing through loss felt impossible.

The maelstrom of my conflicting emotions in the subsequent weeks ranged through guilt, shock, envy, relief, denial, regret, vulnerability, numbness, anxiety, fear, loss of control, insecurity and abandonment. They could all kick off and make me feel I was 'losing it', feeling depressed, ashamed, meaningless, impotent to act or to change anything in my world.

I now know what was happening was all a perfectly normal part of my grieving process. But if I didn't have any life preparation or language to know what was going on, how could I manage it? How could I know it would ever get any better?

My meltdowns

One of my coping mechanisms in loss, whether it was a 'happy loss', such as each of our daughters getting married, or a deeply sad loss, such as a death in the family or even the death of one of our many family pets, had always been to close myself away privately and weep deeply and sometimes uncontrollably. I had never bought into the mantra that big boys don't cry. This one did and still does. So I was accustomed to meltdowns, at least in private. I found them healing and inwardly cleansing.

I also knew that grief could slap you around the face at the most unexpected times with the most innocent of triggers. Like being in the shower and thinking it was a while since I had spoken to my mum, so I should ring her. And only then remembering she had died the previous year. And suddenly I was swept away on a wave of uncontrollable grief and weeping.

What I hadn't expected was the sheer unpredictability and frequency of meltdowns I had, from the moment of Vicky's diagnosis, and then through the first six months or so after her death. Snot and tears were a regular feature of my life, mostly privately but sometimes also in trusted company.

When Vicky was alive, my meltdowns were laced with pain and uncertainty. I was weeping and mourning for someone who was still alive, and whose life could conceivably continue for years through to a state of simple existence and near vegetation. I had a good idea what a death from dementia could look like and I knew it wasn't pretty. I knew Vicky was a fighter who wouldn't give up easily anything she valued, let alone her life. I had no idea how long it would all last, and no one could tell us, especially with such a rare type of dementia. I was both sad with grieving but also stressed by the continuing uncertainty and fear of what tomorrow might bring – yet knowing the inevitability of certain things happening.

Equally I didn't expect my grief to be somehow 'lighter' after her death than before. Another paradox altogether, and I know 'lighter' is the wrong word, but like lots of stuff concerning deep emotions, sometimes we just can't find the right word to express them. Or in the inadequacy of our English language, the right word simply doesn't exist. Anyway, I can't find a better one, so let me explain.

For two days after her death I went to bed weeping, and within minutes of waking up the following morning I was weeping again. On the third morning I woke up and, true to form, I was soon weeping again. Only this time I felt strangely 'light' and unencumbered. My weeping was just as uncontrollable as before, but somehow not so painful or overwhelming. And I realised it was because there was no more uncertainty. We now had some closure. Closure on all the scenarios I had played out in my head about how things might end. And now they had.

It may sound callous to describe it this way, but freedom from the uncertainty was a relief. And that meant I could mourn Vicky's death without thinking about what might or might not happen the next day or the next week or next year. I could stop catastrophising the future and mourn in the present. And that's what I mean by 'lighter'. I was free from the stress of the uncertainty. I even commented to a friend some three months after her death that I felt my life was now free of stress. It was a feeling I cannot ever remember having previously in my adult life. It didn't mean I wasn't still grieving. For a moment I felt guilty that my wife's death had freed me from stress, but I also knew this wasn't one of those tasteless jokes about husbands being free from the stresses of a troublesome wife. I had reached a new stage in my grieving and felt that maybe, after all, the pain would diminish and life could get better.

It didn't mean the meltdowns stopped altogether. They still happened at unexpected times. Like saying prayers with my grandchildren after reading their bedtime stories, naming all the members of the family, including Avo, which was Vicky's chosen name for herself with her grandchildren. And then having to adjust the prayer as she was no longer with us, and just pray for Gaggy (the grandchildren's chosen name for me). Or when someone would refer out of habit to Vicky and Roger. And then correct themselves to say Roger.

While my meltdowns were deeply painful, the measure of my recovery and emergence from the most intense period of grief was, ironically, when I got to the end of a day, or couple of days, and realised I hadn't cried. I felt guilty at first that I hadn't been crying for a couple of days, until I realised the intensity of the pain was reducing. The meltdowns would still happen when I least expected them, but they were becoming less frequent. Frankly, I didn't want to spend the rest of my life as a blubbering wreck at a pity party with my life on hold, and I now realise I used the frequency of my meltdowns as a measure of my progress. Their reduced frequency helped me understand my life wasn't over, and they gave me hope for the future.

To the outside world it may have seemed my meltdowns were signs I wasn't coping well with my loss and I was still in mourning. For me they were essential ingredients in my process of recovery.

You can't judge a book by looking at the cover.

Time to reflect

Please pause for a few minutes before you go on to the next chapter and reflect on a few of the questions that may have arisen for you:

- We all experience loss in life. Has any loss in your life fundamentally affected the way you think about yourself or who you are?
- How have you been able to adapt to your new identity after a grievous loss?
- In the same way that we all experience loss, we all have our coping mechanisms. Mine were emotional meltdowns. Do you know what yours are?
- Do your coping mechanisms help you process the loss? Or do they just help you ignore it?

Chapter Twelve: Beyond the Loss

Looking after myself and coping with the loss of my wife was one thing. Survival is good, but only for a while. Simply surviving would not have been enough. Re-entering and recovering my joy of life and sense of purpose was something else.

In the years after Vicky's diagnosis, I grieved deeply for the loss of the person who was still living.

In the days and months after her death I mourned her death in my grief.

What's the difference between grieving and mourning? David Kessler explains it for me: 'Grief is what's going on inside of us, while mourning is what we do on the outside.'[73] Kessler says that while everyone grieves differently, we all have in common the need for our grief to be witnessed:

> That doesn't mean needing someone to try to lessen it or reframe it for them. The need is for someone to be fully present to the magnitude of their loss without trying to point out the silver lining.[74]

There is an important implication here for how we respond to people who are grieving the loss of a loved one. They may not be mourning in the way you or I might mourn, but their grief may still be deep and painful.

Kessler continues:

> But in our hyperbusy world, grief has been minimised and sanitised ... in our current culture, the mourner is made to feel that though his or her own world has been shattered, everyone else's

---

73 Kessler, *Finding Meaning*, p. 31.

74 Ibid., p. 29.

world goes on as if nothing has changed. There are too few rituals to commemorate mourning and too little time allotted to it.[75]

It isn't the same for every culture. Latin, Middle Eastern and indigenous tribe cultures worldwide have public rituals and customs to mark periods of mourning for the death of loved ones. I recall my experience when living and working in Spain in my early twenties that widows and widowers were expected to wear black or dark colours for a year in mourning after the death of a spouse. Many people in Spain and Portugal still wear black by choice long beyond that period of a year following the death of their loved ones.

Intriguingly we have a National Day of Remembrance in the UK to honour those who lived and died in service of their countries in the Military Forces. Books of Remembrance were created for those who died of COVID-19 in the pandemic. The period of mourning at the death of Queen Elizabeth II in 2022 was an intense and remarkable outpouring of national grief. Yet we have lost many of our historic community, family and personal rituals of mourning for those who are most close to us, our friends and family.

I remember as an eight-year-old child seeing my grandfather laying in rest in his coffin in the living room of his house before his burial, and my grandmother receiving visitors. Friends and family could visit and pay their respects. His was the first dead body I had ever seen. Yet now our custom is for our loved ones to lay in rest in funeral parlours, to be visited by appointment. I don't know why or when we shifted away from those customs and rituals, I can only observe that we have done so and made death something more detached, sanitised and hidden from our everyday lives. Swept under the carpet. Maybe that's part of why we have lost the language for death in our UK culture, and we recoil in horror at the frankly healthier ways of mourning death openly in other cultures.

We don't handle public shows of emotion very well, do we? Unless it's sports, of course, where every and any emotion seem permissible. Maybe we've taken to heart too seriously the saying attributed to the great Bill Shankly,

---

75 Kessler, *Finding Meaning*, p. 30

the legendary Liverpool Football Club manager: 'Some people think football is a matter of life and death. I assure you, it's much more serious than that.'[76]

How do we change that culture?

We start by stopping being so conformist with it. We start by talking about it more openly and by wearing our pain with less stoicism.

Above all, we start accepting that death isn't failure: it's the end of a life that was always going to end at some point, possibly much later, less tragically, suddenly or painfully, but was always destined to end.

The reality of death at some point in our lives doesn't diminish the pain and the grief, but it helps us see the pain and grief as a natural part of life rather than an aberration that has to be hidden or denied. There is no shame in grief. It is perfectly human and now that I have experienced grievous loss, I understand life as incomplete without it.

Hitting the wall

In the immediate weeks after Vicky's death I lost completely my motivation to work. I had worked three days a week for several years, which had given me time and space to look after Vicky as well as looking after myself. My work and work colleagues had played a critical part in helping me look after myself over the previous years.

I took about ten days off when she died and thought I could get back into work OK. And I did for a couple of weeks before I suddenly found I couldn't work anymore. I woke up one Monday morning just not wanting to fulfil any of the meetings or client work scheduled that day. I couldn't concentrate on work. I had always loved my work but was now in 'Why bother?' mode – what difference does it make, why don't I just pack it in? I had lost all motivation, not just for work – but for anything else.

I am going to let my journal tell a bit of the story now.

Three weeks after Vicky died, I wrote:

My emotions have been a total rollercoaster these last two weeks.

---

76 www.brainyquote.com/quotes/bill_shankly_312046 (accessed 4.12.23).

From shock to a sense of unreality, to a sense of release, then to deep loss and emptiness through to combating a complete lack of motivation by returning to work, to lightness again – how bizarre talking about 'light grief' – but it's grief in the moment, rather than the overshadowing grief of the last ten-plus years and the anxiety about what next, how will Vicky be if she recovers from this awful virus?

I have wept every day and today was set off by my pastor's tribute to Vicky in the online church service this morning. He spoke really movingly about her for over four minutes, a genuine tribute. Grief not then made any easier by going and having a second attempt to clear her prayer room – just awful to do, to decide what to keep, what to throw away, what to place with her in the coffin…

Felt drained and off to bed at 9.00 p.m. to write this!

The reality was that I had hit the wall and needed to stop. I took a few weeks off, slept, walked, exercised, wept and basically gave myself the chance to recharge my batteries and start a proper return to life again. I went back to work when I felt ready.

Back to my journal about eight weeks after her death:

Last night I wept uncontrollably for a couple of hours. I had been reading Vicky's letters to me and sorting out some old photos – seeing her in the fullness of her beauty – she was stunningly beautiful all through her life and I felt so much loss and couldn't understand why she left me, why she was taken away.

Then this morning I realised my heart was broken. I realised I had resisted describing myself as broken-hearted and preferred to find words like 'wounded' but now I understood my heart was broken … just recognising and naming it was the start of my healing.

I realised my heart has been broken for years now, all the years of Vicky's decline into dementia, the loss of the young woman, the ageless woman who was my wife and my great love.

Simply writing and acknowledging this pain feels like a release, a flood of emotion and tears, but a necessary release. As to why she has been taken from me, I don't know I'll ever know the answer in this life – so I just have to pop it into the mystery box.

Ten days later my entry reads:

> I realised this morning I hadn't written anything for several days, and that shows how far I've come. The weekly anniversaries of her death and funeral have become less painful and sometimes I've not thought about them until the evening.

After another week:

> Yesterday was ten weeks since Vicky died. I nearly got through the day without crying, until the evening when I was with Ali.
> But today (it's 10.35 p.m.) I've got through a whole day without crying for the first time.
> I've experienced today a weird sense of freedom and lightness – feeling that today was a 'normal' day, working, walking, and free of any responsibility as a carer anymore. I know I haven't had that responsibility for some time, but today I actually *felt* it, feeling I'm in the present moment, not grieving for yesterday or worrying about what tomorrow might bring. Probably helped by a really good night's sleep Saturday to Sunday (ten hours!) and a decent sleep last night too. Been a long time since I've slept well. Or maybe I've slept well because my heart is healing, and I've let go of Vicky. Anyway it feels different today, unburdened and able to get on with life.

Hitting the wall – again!

What I didn't expect was to hit the wall a second time a few months later. Six months after Vicky died, I had a rollercoaster period of ten days of ups and downs. Every day had highs and lows all on the same day.

My journal entry for Friday, 16 October 2020 read:

> Day off work – danced in the morning and wept in the evening when I was walking in the dark by the River Adur. The sadness and tears were so overwhelming I lay down on a bench and had to wait for the pain to subside.

And yet the joy in the week of Rachael's scan for 'wriggler', baby Smith number two.

The following Monday:

Hit the wall in the morning, weeping and couldn't work. Spent most of the morning trying to regain sufficient composure to run my client webinar – and I enjoyed it!

Even got through session five of the Bereavement Journey course for the first time without crying. Rollercoaster day again. What's tomorrow going to hold?

And the Tuesday:

Another weeping episode in the company team stand up meeting this morning and I had to take off the rest of the day and the week.

I was again so grateful for my colleagues giving me the time out I needed to get through and process this new wave of deep grief.

This period coincided with the run-up to Vicky's birthday at the end of October, which would be the first without her. I had no idea at the time whether those occurrences were connected, but I now suspect I was in the stage of depression described by Swiss American psychiatrist Elisabeth Kübler-Ross in her 1969 landmark book *On Death and Dying*.[77]

Depression in this stage mimics clinical depression: 'I'm so sad, why bother with anything?', 'I miss my loved one; why go on?' In this state we can become silent, refuse visitors and spend much of the time mournful and sullen. Which is something else about the journey of grief – it's not all explicable by reasoning on cause and effect.

Sometimes it just is what it is and while we can't explain it, at least

---

77 Elisabeth Kübler-Ross, *On Death and Dying* (New York: The Macmillan Company, 1969). Kübler-Ross originally developed five stages to describe the process patients with terminal illness go through as they come to terms with their own deaths; it was later applied to grieving friends and family as well, who seemed to undergo a similar process. The stages describe a series of emotions experienced by people who are grieving: denial, anger, bargaining, depression and acceptance (DABDA). Kübler-Ross herself subsequently recognised the stages aren't necessarily linear or of equal intensity or duration.

now I know that I wasn't 'losing it' and that my emotions were perfectly normal.

Weeping and dancing

Let me say a bit more about the unpredictability of this period of mourning as I experienced it.

The journal entry of 16 October may have mystified you a bit where it talks about dancing in the morning and weeping in the evening. Let me explain.

One morning during those first six months, I found myself doing what others would describe as a 'dad dance' as I listened to some upbeat music in my bedroom.

It wasn't like I decided suddenly 'I have to stop mourning and embrace life', but allowing myself to do the things I enjoyed again was a really important step to help work through my grief and back into life.

I had forgotten my grief momentarily. And then I felt guilty for forgetting Vicky's death, and asked myself what I was doing. How on earth can I be dancing when my wife is dead?

The Toploader hit at the turn of the century captures how dancing is 'a supernatural delight':[78]

You can't dance and stay uptight,
It's such a supernatural delight.

That was the point I realised I could weep *and* dance, and it wasn't disrespectful to Vicky but it was OK. I didn't love or miss her any less, but the joy and simple pleasure of music and dance had started to return to my heart and soul.

I love music. I grew up in Liverpool in the era of The Beatles, so I'm more inclined to a bit of rock and roll, jazz and blues than to classical music.

Contemporary worship music got me through the decade or so of the journey with Vicky and the period of intense grieving. In that period, I

---

78 'Dancing in the Moonlight' written by Sherman Kelly. Copyright © 1970 EMI U Catalog Inc. EMI United Partnership Limited. All rights reserved.

would go to bed in the hope (rather than the expectation) of sleeping without tossing and turning for hours, playing worship music low on a Bluetooth speaker until I would eventually fall asleep. They were my lullabies.

A couple of months later, and in hindsight, a sign that I was through the intense period of grief, I found myself returning to the music of my twenties. My music-streaming channel introduced me to a whole generation of music I had missed. Which is why you may spot quotations from the likes of Coldplay and Snow Patrol. Don't judge me if their stuff is not to your liking – and don't pity me for taking so long to discover their music either. My point is that their songs about the human condition started to give me a fresh way of thinking about my life and the specific circumstances I faced. It felt like my soul was re-engaging with life and the things I enjoyed.

A few days after my first dad dance in the privacy of my bedroom (fully clothed by the way, lest your imagination spoils your lunch), I was walking to the shops where I live in Steyning, feeling at peace with the world and smiling – when I found myself thinking I had to put on my sad face to go into the local Co-op. And then I asked myself, why? Who was I putting my sad face on for? Why did I feel compelled to think I had to look mournful and unhappy when the sun was shining and I was feeling OK?

It was these moments when I realised I was trying to fit my feelings and demeanour into the mourning mode I thought was most socially appropriate. I was allowing my impression of external expectations of my grieving to rule over me. I was trying to behave in a way I thought other people might expect me to behave, even though I wasn't feeling the way I thought they might expect of me. How weird and irrational is that? Why?

It was a tipping point for me. I realised I was emerging from the intense period of grief and mourning when everything in life had been coloured by my loss. To paraphrase Coldplay, I had started dancing when the lights had gone out. The lights were still out because I was missing Vicky deeply. But there is still joy in dancing and joy to be had in life when I allowed myself to live in the present moment.

There is joy to be had in laughter too. Watching a good comedy on the television was balm to my soul. A few weeks earlier I might have thought such things frivolous and meaningless. But now I was finding pleasure in them again, discovering there is joy in the simple things of life even after loss. I had started feeling safe again.

My sense of joy and meaning had started to grow again after my loss. It sounds perverse I know, but Joni Mitchell sang the truth in 'Big Yellow Taxi':

Don't it always seem to go
That you don't know what you've got 'til it's gone.[79]

When we have had loving relationships and lose them, we can decide to go one of three ways:

- We can decide either that the loss was too painful, and we don't want to experience such loss again.
- We can decide to be guarded about our relationships and never go deep because we have seen the pain of loss in others.
- Or we can decide the experience of love was so fulfilling that it's worth the pain to truly appreciate the joy again. And live fully again.

I knew which path Vicky would have chosen for me. I have chosen the third way. At the time of writing, I don't know how that will turn out, but hey, that's life.

Settling into new patterns of life

Finding new and stable patterns in life was really important for Vicky in the latter stages of her life. After her death it was my turn to seek out and find the patterns that suited me.

Caring for Vicky at home meant a constant readjustment of my patterns and habits, new routines that gave my life shape. There was a routine for when she was living at home that I lost when she went into a care home, and I had to adopt a different routine.

I remember the emotional impact of grocery shopping immediately after she had gone into care, going to the supermarket shelves and putting in my basket the regular foods she would eat – and then realising someone

---

79 'Big Yellow Taxi' written by Joni Mitchell. Copyright © 1970 Crazy Crow Music. Administered by Sony/ATV Music Publishing. All rights reserved.

else was feeding her now and she wouldn't be able to eat the things I was buying. It took a few trips to the shops to settle into a new routine, not having to put things back on the supermarket shelf, and realise I only had to buy the things *I* needed and not the things *we* needed.

When she went into care, my life patterns changed and revolved around visiting, coordinating visits for other people, keeping friends and family up to date with how she was. I no longer had to plan support for her at home when I went out for client work or to visit friends and family. It was a bittersweet new freedom.

And when she died, I had to find a set of routines that were no longer shaped by an interdependent relationship with my wife but were shaped by my need to live an independent life. In one way I was now free to do what I wanted the way I wanted. I was free to cook and eat what I wanted when I wanted. I was free to come and go from home as and when I wanted. In one sense a whole set of new freedoms had come into my life almost unnoticed. Sounds great, doesn't it? And yet the price of those freedoms was the terrible pain of my loss, a yawning gap in my life and a great big hole in my heart.

In many respects this is where the rubber really hit the road in my experience of loss. The challenge was whether to get comfortable in my independence and create routines for myself that would protect me from life, or was I prepared for my routines to be disrupted, and embrace a new phase of life? Even in the intense period of grief I chose to explore the latter route.

I was given the very good advice from a friend who had lost her husband tragically and unexpectedly five years earlier to make sure I didn't isolate myself but ensure I got out and saw friends and family. I had to be selective about where I went and who I saw.

At this stage I could only be with people who had been alongside me in the journey and didn't need explanations for how I was, but it was still a conscious effort of the will to accept an invitation out to supper, for example, when my natural preference would have been to stay at home with a bottle of wine and Netflix for company.

Being selective about the people I saw was a way of being kind to myself.

Because of the pandemic I couldn't return to my church for more than a year. To be honest, I had dreaded the idea of going to church and being among such a large group of people who knew and loved Vicky. We knew so many people and the idea of being consoled by them all was simply overwhelming. I couldn't have faced them. In fact, it was just over a year before I went to a Sunday service in person, by which time I could at least manage to speak complete sentences without melting down in tears, primarily because I had had time to process my grief and complete my mourning. And that's another difference I found between grief and mourning. My mourning felt complete, but the grief of my loss would always be with me.

Be kind to yourself

Looking after myself through the whole experience was critical to my well-being. But now I had to be kind to myself as well to move beyond the loss and appreciate life again.

By being kind to myself I don't mean being self-indulgent. Indeed, sometimes it meant denying myself the self-indulgence I wanted instinctively. As a concrete example I recall a moment when I chose to play one of my favourite blues albums in the car, only to find that within minutes my mood had dipped seriously to the point that I had lost concentration. Not quite so bad as being in the outside lane of the motorway and having a meltdown, but enough for me to spot that I was spiralling and had to switch to some more upbeat and 'hopeful' music so as to regain control of my driving.

Effectively I was switching my thinking and emotions from a negative to a positive cycle, and after a few minutes it worked and restored my emotional balance. I was noticing my sadness but thinking that driving my car was not a good place to allow it to go deeper. It wasn't denial of my sadness, but care for myself to reduce the risk for me and other drivers on the road.

I knew it was OK to allow myself to be sad and feel my loss when it happened naturally and was outside my control. But I also discovered that it was not helpful to feed or trigger the pain unnecessarily when I had a choice and was still able to exercise some control.

The thing with grief and triggers is that everyone reacts differently to the things they experience, and there are no one-size-fits-all solutions. For example, Vicky and I had several favourite walking routes and I still walk them all. They do trigger memories, and while I may find them wistful,

I can smile at them and do not find them overwhelming. On the other hand, I know there are people who would have to avoid those same routes because the memories are far too painful.

I have friends and even family who could not enter our house for over a year after Vicky died, and wept even as they stood at the front door. Others were glad to come in and remind themselves of her presence and her paintings and photographs on the walls.

I'm not saying don't play blues music if you want, or follow the routes you went together, but please be aware of your circumstances and how it may affect your mood. Especially when operating dangerous machinery like a car!

Another way of caring for myself was to let people into my pain. Not always in the moment because sometimes it was too intense, and I would be incoherent. But after the event it helped me just to share it – I didn't need anyone to fix me, I just needed a hug or touch to let me know they cared. Back to that thing about being present for someone in their pain and grief.

Anticipating the anniversaries

One of the things I dreaded was the first cycle of annual events and anniversaries. My first birthday without her. The first of her birthdays after her death. The first Christmas without her. The first anniversary of her death. I had been warned to prepare and plan for them and ensure there was something to mark them, to ensure I wasn't alone, but never to ignore them and hope they would just pass by unnoticed. I was glad we had plans in place and could celebrate her life on each occasion with both tears and laughter.

On her first birthday since her death, my daughters and I watched the movie *Calendar Girls* together with copious wine and our favourite takeaway food, remembering how Vicky had been in stitches during the film and got hilariously drunk for the only time ever in our girls' memory. Only thing was that I had forgotten completely that the storyline behind the film was the tragic loss of a husband from cancer, and it was meltdown time again for me. In retrospect, not the best choice of film for the occasion, but we wanted to remember her laughter and joy as well as the sadness of the occasion.

The first anniversary of her death fell on a Monday, which was a workday for friends and family as well as me. We marked it intentionally with a lunch on the Sunday instead with my sister-in-law Lotty and her husband, Chris, and enjoyed a surprise visit by some friends who came with flowers to mark the occasion before I went over to family in the evening. All of which meant the anniversary was intentionally marked. Again, we had celebrated Vicky's life with tears and laughter, and the anniversary itself, the following day, went by like any other day.

I had thought I had got through the first annual cycle with the anniversary of her death. I thought that first cycle was complete and I had survived. I thought the first year was ticked off the calendar. The first Christmas, the first Easter, the first family holiday together, all the family birthdays without her were done. They were all ticked off.

Only the cycle wasn't complete after all. I had not allowed for the first anniversary of her funeral, and that was the most unexpected and painful of them all. I just wasn't ready for that one until the day arrived and I had absolutely no plans in place in anticipation of the painful memories that came flooding in. The absence of a plan was not a good plan! That was a meltdown day I had not bargained for.

Expect the unexpected

The unexpected pain of the first anniversary of Vicky's funeral was a real and overwhelming surprise.

However, not all my unexpected experiences were so unpleasant.

Vicky's death had released me from stress. I didn't have the uncertainty anymore of not knowing how long this was all going to last. I didn't have the uncertainty of how her life was going to end. I didn't have the uncertainty of how painful her last days or months would be for her, whether it would be a long and lingering death as the life drained slowly out of her, unable to speak or eat or drink independently. I didn't have to worry about what she was doing or how she was. I didn't have the dread of discovering something new on each of my visits – the knowledge that my presence might disturb or stress her. I didn't have the stress of thinking the care staff were keeping the reality of her condition and behaviour from me to protect me.

Her life had now ended. There was a dreadful finality to it all. My anxieties created by all the uncertainty, my internal monologues, my worst fears and imaginations about how the end might come, had all evaporated. They no longer overshadowed my life and I was free from them.

My deep pain and grief were accompanied by a new freedom from stress and anxiety. Of course, I could have found other new things to be anxious about, but why would I do that to myself?

This freedom from stress was something new that I had never experienced as an adult. I can find no English word to describe it, but it felt like the complete *shalom* of the Jewish tradition – the total peace of mind, body and spirit all working in harmonious well-being. I feel both guilty writing this and fearful of being misjudged for describing it. Had I been secretly wishing she were dead and relieved now she was gone? How could I possibly be feeling such deep grief at the loss of my wife and total peace at the same time? How can both be true when they appear so contradictory? And yet that's where I found myself.

I told a trusted friend that I suddenly felt free of stress and it was amazingly liberating simply to admit it to someone who knew how deeply Vicky and I had loved each other, and who would listen to me without judgement. It was also completely unexpected. I had never foreseen a time when I would be free of anxiety and some form of stress. It felt like a gift to grasp and not to reject out of guilt or fear of judgement.

This new sense of freedom didn't deny the reality of my grief or my loss. They had not diminished. Vicky had not diminished in my memory of her. But now I realised I could grasp the peace that was in my reach, if only I didn't beat myself up for reaching out for it.

Time to reflect

Like so much in life, we can't control or plan for the unexpected. When it arrives, we can, however, choose how we see and experience it. We don't have to experience it all as a victim of circumstance. We have choice in how we respond in times of great adversity *and* in times of joy.

Here are a few more questions for you to think about:

- How well would you say you look after yourself after experiencing loss?
- How do you handle the anniversaries that inevitably come after bereavements of loved ones – have they marked significantly the way you spend those days, especially when they coincide with events like Christmas or New Year?
- How well prepared do you think you are to face the unexpected in life and survive it well?

Chapter Thirteen: Coping with Loss – Looking After Me

Loss is part of our human condition. A painful part we don't want to live with, but life isn't life without it.

When Vicky was diagnosed with dementia, I had to admit the brutal reality that dementia can be a terminal condition. It meant we could be in this for the long haul or the short haul. And I had better be ready for either. So I had better look after myself.

I know it sounds selfish. How could I think about looking after myself when I was losing my wife so slowly and painfully? Shouldn't I have been putting her first and squeezing every drop I could from our remaining time together?

The answer to both questions is yes. It's and-and not either-or. Isn't it ironic that when we are going through difficult stuff, we are told by all around us to look after ourselves? So, we do. Then we think we are being selfish and feel guilty. But if the grief journey teaches you nothing else, it's that we humans are full of contradictions, and it's best to accept them as part of our human condition rather than try too hard to fight them.

To be honest, I didn't have to be told to look after myself or cajoled into some self-care regime. I knew instinctively that if I was going to be able to look after Vicky for the indeterminate long run we faced, I would be of little use to her or the rest of our family if I crashed and burned with exhaustion. It's a bit like the advice on the plane: put on your own oxygen mask before you try to help anyone else, even if it's your own family.

Have you ever noticed we humans can be both Homer Simpson and *Star Trek*'s Mr Spock all in the same day? We are a bunch of rational, spiritual, emotional, logical, illogical, biased and hormonal beings, all rolled into an envelope of skin and bones. We are capable of the most noble endeavours and inflicting injuries and offences all in the same twenty-four hours.

I had to face the reality that my external envelope of skin and bones contains a whole person made up of the three big dimensions of body, soul and spirit. And to complicate matters even more, my soul has its own splinter group where my will frequently has to choose between my conflicting thoughts and emotions. When things are going my way they feel like the best jazz trios, with sax, drums and piano all in tune and in sync, ready to improvise and play both collectively and solo as the rhythm leads.

At other times my body, soul and spirit or my thoughts, emotions and will compete with each other and are out of sync, pulling in equal and opposite directions, playing the wrong notes at the wrong time. Sometimes they seem to shout, 'Choose me! choose me!' like three warring siblings. Or two of them gang up on the third to shut them down and keep them in their place, or declare a truce that I know I will pay for in the end. That way I can enjoy a few minutes of peace and quiet. Until one of the warring siblings breaks the truce.

What we really need is for them all to get on together and play in harmony. And therein lies the secret of our well-being. I know of no English word to describe that sense of balance and well-being regardless of the circumstances and what is kicking off around and within you. The word 'peace' doesn't quite capture it.

I find it's the Middle Eastern languages that have more expressive vocabulary for this idea of well-being and wholeness. In Hebrew it's *shalom*, in Arabic it's *salaam*, *sliem* in Maltese, *shlama* in Syriac-Assyrian and *sälam* in Ethiopian Semitic languages. It means peace, harmony, wholeness, completeness, prosperity, welfare and tranquillity. But how can we get that longed-for *shalom*?

Start with our habits

Examining our habits seems a strange place to start. But in Hebrews 12:11 we read:

> No discipline seems pleasant at the time, but painful. Later on, however, it produces a harvest of righteousness and peace for those who have been trained by it.

A harvest of righteousness and peace sounds to me like a good proxy for *shalom*.

We are disciplined as children to help us distinguish between right and wrong, what is and what is not acceptable. Through discipline we learn habits and 'rules for life' that become ingrained in our daily routines. We continue to learn through adulthood and develop new disciplines and habits that we think will benefit us in the short or longer terms, either because they give us pleasure, because they are good for our health and well-being, or because they will help us avoid pain or punishment. The downside is that we can get stuck in our habits, and we forget why we have them in the first place.

Our habits carry a hidden cost. We only have so many hours in a day, and our habits often mean that we have to sacrifice things that would make life so much easier and pleasurable in the moment if we dropped them. That slice of cake instead of an apple, the extra glass of wine because we feel a bit blue, an extra half hour in bed because we went to bed at 1.00 a.m. because of a riveting film on Netflix. Relaxing our disciplines for a day or so might feel sweet, but then we start to drop them because it didn't do us too much harm to relax them for a day or so.

Disciplines can feel like a bit of a killjoy. Where's the joy in life if we take away its simple pleasures? Like so much else, it comes back to how we see life, how we spend our time, and the search for the sweet spot where disciplines create joy. I had always enjoyed running, for example, and found it a great relief for stress. After putting on a bit too much weight, I found running to be hard basically because my heart, muscles and joints were carrying too much extra load. I disciplined myself about my diet, lost some weight and suddenly running became easier and more pleasurable again.

When I reflect on the pattern of my days, I realise so much of it is habitual and has developed over time to the point where it has become essential to my daily and weekly rhythms of life. Much depends, of course, on our stage of life, childcare and work patterns that determine when and where we have to be at certain times. There are parts of my day that I can control and there are parts of my day that I cannot directly control.

Our disciplines are formed in those parts of our day, however short or long, where we have choice. Earlier I referred to my daily discipline of devotional time with God. In my early days of walking with the Lord, I recall hearing advice that I should be spending time with God every morning. Working in a demanding and busy job with three young children meant that even five minutes a day sounded like a big stretch, but that was where I started. I adjusted my alarm clock incrementally, and in time five minutes became fifteen minutes and fifteen minutes became twenty minutes and twenty minutes became half an hour. I took that extra time willingly because of the benefits that I experienced, and now I cannot start the day without that time because it puts me in a place of peace so I can face the day, whatever challenges it might bring.

Through my journey with Vicky, I had to adapt my disciplines to take care of myself in all of the dimensions of body, spirit and soul. After her death it was enormously tempting to give up on many of those disciplines, and so I faced a set of choices. This next section is all about the choices I made so that I could continue to grow in life and not to give up.

Stretch to grow

One of the key things I learned under the weight of stress and pressure both before and after Vicky's death was the importance of stretching myself in one way or another either physically, intellectually or spiritually. Cue Coldplay: 'Under this pressure, under this weight, we are diamonds taking shape.'[80]

In grief it is all too easy and tempting to give up on growing and learning. We are under pressure; we are being squeezed unbearably.

If you are a bit of a nerd on Improvement methods you will be familiar with the Japanese term *Kaizen*, made famous in the world of manufacturing by Toyota with their ground-breaking work in the second half of the twentieth century, which in turn gave birth to the 'lean' technology and a plethora of organisation improvement methods.

Now, you might ask what on earth have Toyota and lean manufacturing principles got to do with grief? Bear with me a little longer...

---

80 'Adventure of a Lifetime' written by Guy Berryman, Jonathan Buckland, William Champion, Chris Martin, Tor Erik Hermansen and Mikkel Eriksen. Copyright © 2015 Universal Music Publishing MGB Ltd and EMI Music Publishing Ltd. All rights reserved.

In brief, *Kaizen* has three big elements:[81]

- Continuous improvement, often through small 'baby' steps, where workers were constantly challenging their own working methods and environment and implementing a series of continuous incremental minor improvement steps in their workplace.
- Renewal. This is referred to in business English as innovation or disruption. It is a radical departure or transformation and is much more than the sum of the small gradual improvements.
- Sustainability. This state refers to an organisation being able to sustain any improvement it accomplishes as a foundation for the next improvement push. If an organisation is resistant to change for the better and always falls back to its original state, then it cannot sustain any change and hence any effort put into driving *Kaizen* would be worthless.

Interestingly, the approach was called 'lean' since it refers to an organisation like a body, where a healthy one is lean and with little spare fat, versus an unhealthy body that has lots of waste and fat to trim. Are you getting my drift?

Maybe it's the circles of life I move in and the company I keep, but I have yet to meet anyone who does not want to live a healthy life. We don't all manage to do so, often for reasons outside of our personal control, including the genetic hand we are dealt. I've also met plenty of people with self-destructive habits, people who say they want to change their lifestyles but somehow just can't carry their New Year resolution to take more exercise, eat, smoke or drink less past 31 January. But I still haven't met anyone who welcomed developing cancer, diabetes, dementia or heart disease. We all want to live healthy lives. Yet we have to live with what Kessler says when he wrote 'loss is simply what happens to you in life. Meaning is what you make happen.'[82]

My take is that the *Kaizen* principles and mindset apply as much to our personal lives as they do to organisational or manufacturing life. I am not

---

81 My summary.

82 Kessler, *Finding Meaning*, p. 7.

saying we should think of ourselves as a mechanical assembly line, but I am referring to the mindset that looks for continuous improvement in the way we live. Why else would you buy that new product to stop your hair thinning, or go on that miracle slimming diet? The human desire to want to improve constantly, or at least preserve well our lives, is the fuel that drives marketing and sales machinery the world over. That plus fear.

In my everyday thinking, to stretch myself to grow is basically a mini-me of the *Kaizen* mindset. Regularly challenging myself about why I feel what I feel, why I think what I think, why I believe what I believe. It's not a process of beating myself up or blaming myself for thinking a specific way. I'm not a masochist. It's just a healthy questioning and curiosity about how I see the world and what I'm learning from my experience of grieving and grief.

Equally, I'm not in la-la land denying the experience of my grief or the horrible circumstances surrounding Vicky's death. They happened and I can't change a thing about them, however much I wish they had been different. Grievous loss is a fundamental part of life. It's how we deal with it that determines how healthily we live the rest of our lives.

Stretching ourselves might feel a bit overwhelming in such circumstances, but I found it to be a crucial part of being kind to myself. What do I mean in practical terms? What does this stretching malarkey actually look like? Is it as painful as it sounds?

Stretching the body

This isn't meant to be narcissistic, but let's start with the easy one in the jazz ensemble, the one we can all see in the mirror. Maybe it's not so easy looking in the mirror, but it is the physically visible bit. And, inconvenient though it may be, it's the bit I can measure and weigh. It is, after all, the temple of the Holy Spirit[83] if we want to get biblical about it.

I had to persuade myself that tape measures, weighing scales and blood pressure monitors are not tools of the devil created to terrorise me and make me feel bad about myself. They are inanimate objects that help me measure

---

83 1 Corinthians 6:19-20: 'Do you not know that your bodies are temples of the Holy Spirit, who is in you, whom you have received from God? You are not your own; you were bought at a price. Therefore honour God with your bodies.'

myself. And even though I far prefer to keep them in the cupboard out of sight and mind, they do give me some helpful data when I occasionally bring them out into the light.

I wasn't unhealthy and I wasn't particularly unfit for my age. I thought I was in reasonable nick. However, I knew the next few years were likely to take a toll physically as well as emotionally if I was going to care for Vicky well.

Cutting to the chase, I took my courage in my hands and engaged with the measuring things and decided that I needed to improve my fitness. That meant determining to do some pretty simple stuff. I know, I know... simple to say, not so simple to do.

But don't worry, I'm not here to give you tips on looking after yourself physically through exercise and diet or indulge in any 'look at me' stuff. There are people far better qualified for that than me.

Let's just say that I built on the health-building things I enjoyed already and limited the stuff that I knew was less good for me. Good physical health is not rocket science. It is the basic equation between healthy calories in and calories out. I boil it down to finding the right balance between a good, tasty and pleasurable diet to maintain a healthy immune system, and enjoyable exercise to boost the strength of my heart and muscles. I take special pleasure knowing the antioxidants in red wine are helping my immune system!

The crucial thing was not just knowing what I had to do, but having the motivation to do it. And I had a double dose of motivation.

I appreciated that we could be in this for the long run and so I needed all the physical reserves and psychological energy I could muster. I couldn't afford to get sick. I had witnessed Vicky's family's double loss of both parents in the space of two years and their overwhelming grief. I resolved that, to the extent that I could prevent it, that double loss would not happen in my family.

And that's the thing here. *Knowing* how to look after myself physically wasn't the issue. Frankly, however hard it is, it's the member of the trio you and I know most about and probably invest most time and money on. The issue was the motivation and determination to do so. Out of the motivation I could find the disciplines, and with the disciplines I eventually forged a set of new habits one step at a time.

Joe Wicks made his name keeping the UK fit during the pandemic. All those stretches. Painful at first but easier every day. Joe taught well-researched health benefits to stretching our muscles, but there is also a different kind of stretching, however, that benefits us physically.

Nassim Taleb, the author of *The Black Swan*,[84] describes himself in *Antifragile* as 'an intellectual who has the appearance of a bodyguard'.[85] Since you were about to ask, he says he developed his physique to ward off physical threats following the 2008 banking crisis and *The Wall Street Journal* advising him to 'stock up on bodyguards'.[86] He decided instead that it was cheaper to look like one himself and he hired a trainer whose method was the 'maximum lifts' type of training. It basically consists of short episodes in the gym in which he focused solely on improving his previous maximum weight in a single lift. The workout was limited to trying to exceed the previous mark once or twice rather than spending lots of time on repetitions. The result was that his body grew to anticipate that it would need to deadlift, say, 5lbs more than he did last time.

Apart from the weird insight into the mind of a self-styled radical philosopher, the point here is that Taleb incessantly stretched his physical capacity to lift weights and transformed his body over time with small incremental steps one day at a time.

In practical terms, Vicky and I already had a routine of daily walks with our dogs, and I had a daily exercise regime for my back after experiencing back pain in my early thirties. I simply built on what I was already doing, and to stretch myself I would regularly add little increments or additions. Another ten seconds for this, another two repetitions for that, add a new exercise, and over the course of a year the small steps mounted up into something that would have been impossible to sustain a year earlier. And that's the point. Continuously stretching what I did (as well as literally stretching and lifting weights during the exercises) gave me energy not only to care for Vicky but also to come through 'leaner' in a healthy way.

---

84 Nassim Nicholas Taleb, *The Black Swan* (New York: Random House, 2010).

85 Nassim Nicholas Taleb, *Antifragile* (New York: Penguin Books, 2012), pp. 46-47.

86 www.wsj.com/articles/SB123457658749086809 (accessed 15.12.23).

Stretching the soul

I think the soul is the instrument in the trio that is the most difficult to play and keep in sync with the others.

What is the soul? In many religious, philosophical, and mythological traditions, the soul is the intangible essence of a living being.

It's that messy mix of stuff that makes us who we are in the eyes of the world, regardless of how we look on the outside. It's our intelligence, our will, choices, mental abilities, reason, emotions, character, feelings, thoughts, personality, behaviours, identity, history, experiences, memories and consciousness. It's often referred to as our 'self'.

For the sake of simplicity, let's break it down into the three elements of our emotions, our thought life and our will. Sticking with the jazz metaphor, this is where the soul can mix things up spontaneously, any of the three different instruments can be heard loudest, and you're never quite sure which one it's going to be from one moment to the next.

Let's start with the emotions. The overlaps with our thought life and will (especially our ability to choose) will become apparent in the process.

Managing our emotions

The emotions are the key place to start when it comes to looking after our soul at times of loss and unbearable stress. Switchfoot get it (again!): 'I've been thinking maybe I've been partly cloudy, maybe I'm the chance of rain.'[87] At times of loss or fear of loss, the emotions mess us up. They refuse to obey reason – and yet they are understandable. They make us lose sleep – and yet they fatigue us, drain our physical energy and make us feel sleepy. They affect what we eat and drink. They make us eat and drink for comfort – and yet they starve us of food and drink through lack of appetite or thirst. They are unpredictable and sometimes unmanageable. They vary from person to person. And our capacity to manage them differs from personality types to gender to social conditioning to culture.

---

87 'Stars' written by Jonathan Foreman. Copyright © 2005 Meadowgreen Music Company. Administered by Capital CMG Publishing. All rights reserved.

Doubtless I will use some sweeping generalisations here, and there will be exceptions to the rules, but I'd like to suggest some common truths to help us cope with loss ourselves and help others to cope with their losses.

It is a shocking reality that in recent years suicide accounts for more than 700,000 deaths a year globally,[88] there is an average 56,000 deaths in the European Union every year,[89] and 6,000 people die from suicide every year in the UK.[90] According to the House of Commons Library suicide statistics report of December 2022: 'The risk of suicide in England and Wales is highest among people aged between 45 and 54 and lowest among people aged under 20 and over 70.'[91]

While every suicide is a tragedy, the evidence around men is particularly alarming. Women across Europe are more likely to attempt suicide or be diagnosed with a mental health condition like depression, yet men account for around three-quarters of all suicides. The gender pattern is the same in the UK as in Europe as a whole. Three-quarters of deaths from suicide in England and Wales involve men, and men aged forty-five to sixty-four have the highest rate of suicide by age.

Generalising across all cases of suicide isn't always helpful, but there are many possibilities that might explain why men are struggling.

The following extract from the website of the Priory Group, an independent provider of mental healthcare in the UK, describes well the male culture and dynamics that I experienced growing up:

> For generations, societal roles have pressured men to 'man up'. They're encouraged to be tough, and any admittance that you're not ok is one of weakness. While women are often wrongly characterised as 'emotional', men are not encouraged to speak up at all. It has its roots in childhood, when we're told that boys don't cry.[92]

---

88 www.who.int/publications/i/item/9789240026643 (accessed 4.12.23).

89 https://ec.europa.eu/eurostat/web/products-eurostat-news/-/ddn-20180716-1 (accessed 4.12.23).

90 https://commonslibrary.parliament.uk/research-briefings/cbp-7749/ (accessed 4.12.23).

91 https://commonslibrary.parliament.uk/research-briefings/cbp-7749/ (accessed 4.12.23).

92 www.priorygroup.com/blog/why-are-suicides-so-high-amongst-men (accessed 4.12.23).

In the Priory Group blog, Dr Natasha Bijlani discusses the outdated idea of what it means to be a man:

> Traditionally, men have been less likely to seek support for mental health issues. This is probably for a number of reasons including stigma and the traditional 'strong male' stereotype still prevalent in our society – the idea that expressing emotion is a sign of weakness.

Do we really have to wait until men own up to thoughts of suicide to help deal with the emotions of loss in life?

We have to shift the dial in our culture and allow men to understand that losses are a normal part of life and not judgements condemning them as failures. And while that sounds a big ask, we can make a start by helping men develop their emotional literacy, particularly in circumstances of loss.

I saw my father-in-law give up on life after losing his wife to cancer in her mid-fifties, and so a family tragedy became a double tragedy within two years. He didn't develop any addictions, but as with so many men, the cornerstones of his life were his family and his business. The friendships he had were generally through his wife with other couples rather than his own, or with business associates. He was also of a generation that tended to protect their children from some of the uglier truths of life, including their own health and emotional challenges. He wasn't to be blamed – his was a generation who lived and fought through the Second World War for our freedom, and who would see personal vulnerability as a threat to their own existence, as a weakness for an enemy to exploit.

I tell you something about my father-in-law because his story may be typical of his generation, and of so many men today whose role models, whether their fathers or grandfathers, knew personal vulnerability as weakness and a threat to their very lives. They raised sons to believe personal and emotional vulnerability are the antithesis of manhood. While they may have been right to adopt that self-protective approach in times of war, it is ironically a pattern that does not serve men so well in the times of peace for which they fought and sacrificed their lives.

Let's look at differences in how men and women deal with emotions and begin with some of the insights offered in the John Gray pop culture classic of 1993, *Men Are From Mars, Women Are From Venus*.[93] Even if you have never read it, I bet you have heard the title. It's one of those book titles that capture an idea, like *Catch-22*[94] or *The Tipping Point*,[95] and shape how we think about the world. Book titles that capture the *zeitgeist* of an era. Sorry about the *zeitgeist* word. I just fancied using it instead of saying 'spirit of the age', which sounds so less learned and much more Hawkwind and space rock for those of a certain age – and yes, there was indeed a musical genre called space rock and a band called Hawkwind. But I digress.

One of the major ideas in Gray's book is about the difference in the way the genders react to stress. Gray states when male tolerance to stressful situations is exceeded, they withdraw temporarily, 'retreating into their cave', so to speak. Often, they literally retreat, for example, to the garage or to go spend time with friends. In their 'caves', men are not necessarily focused on the problem at hand. Yet Gray describes this 'time-out' as helping men distance themselves from the problem, allowing them to re-examine the problem later from a fresh perspective.

Gray holds that when women become unduly stressed, their natural reaction is to talk with someone close about it, even if talking doesn't provide a practical solution to the problem at hand.

Gray's stereotypes may be theoretically faulty for psychology purists, but he reportedly sold 15 million copies[96] with what was considered by CNN[97] as the highest-ranked work of non-fiction in the 1990s. Not bad really for some pop culture allegedly based on flawed theory. But I digress again.

I think Gray's descriptions of different reactions to stress can apply to personality types as well as gender. Introverts and extroverts are neither better nor worse than each other at dealing with stress. The difference between them is they just happen to get their energy for life in completely different but equally valid ways. Introverts tend to want to process internally

---

93 John Gray, *Men Are From Mars, Women Are From Venus* (New York: Harper Collins, 1992).

94 Joseph Heller, *Catch-22* (New York: Simon & Schuster, 1961).

95 Malcolm Gladwell, *The Tipping Point* (Boston, MA: Little Brown, 2000).

96 www.harpercollins.com.au/9780007152599/men-are-from-mars-women-are-from-venus/ (accessed 18.12.23).

97 https://web.archive.org/web/20120908181659/http://articles.cnn.com/1999-12-31/entertainment/1990.sellers_1_book-sales-cumulative-sales-copies?_s=PM:books (accessed 2.1.24).

and quietly by themselves while extroverts tend to process through social interaction and thinking out loud with others.

The central point, however, is that men and women, and introverts and extroverts, broadly speaking, deal with loss in different ways. And some of those ways can be much more damaging than others for our mental and physical health and well-being.

Please hold your objections to my sweeping generalities because there will always be exceptions. But one generality most people hold to be true is that women are better equipped to name, act on and deal with emotions than men. Whether it's conditioning, culture, life experience, career, family expectations or whatever, men don't 'do' emotions as well as women.

Why is that important? Working with loss is about dealing with our emotions, not with our reason. Grievous loss is not something we can fix or reason away. There is no screwdriver or spanner we can use or magic bullet we can fire to fix it.

One of the ways I have found meaning from losing Vicky has been to lead bereavement courses. Some personal evidence about the differing reactions of men and women to grief is that roughly three-quarters of the people at the first few courses I co-facilitated were women. To stay with the anecdotal evidence, the proportion of men attending the courses started to increase dramatically as we socialised and normalised the issue of loss and more men started to role model genuine masculine vulnerability, and to recommend the course to other men.

The consequences of being unable to name and process our emotions, whether caused by gender, personality type, conditioning or whatever, are far-reaching in their consequences for our mental health and physical welfare.

In true blokey fashion, I'll draw the analogy of recovery from loss as a bit like mixing concrete. It needs lots of different ingredients to bind together to make a solid article.

One of the key elements to the mix is having trusting human relationships. There are other elements such as our worldview, but for now let's stick to the point about relationships.

In a post on the *Psychology Today* website, Ronald Riggio writes about the similarities and differences between male-male and female-female friendships. He says that while the similarities tend to outweigh the differences, there are some interesting ways that men's friendships differ from women's:

The most common finding is that men's friendships tend to be more 'instrumental' and less emotional, while women are much more likely than men to share emotions and feelings. Men's friendships are often based on shared activities (e.g., poker or golfing buddies), and are more 'transactional' – reciprocating favours and working together on projects. In other words, men share activities, women share feelings.

On the whole women tend to invest more time and energy in maintaining their friendships – calling friends regularly, meeting more frequently, etc. Men, on the other hand, don't feel as much need to stay in touch.[98]

If my experience is anything to go by, I would add that father-son and mother-daughter relationships tend to work in similar ways.

As a child my brothers and I were taught that boys don't cry. It was OK for my sister to cry. It was OK for my mum to cry. But not for my dad. And not for us. It wasn't simply a parental thing, it was all around us. At school a boy would be bullied mercilessly if he cried. You had to live out the anthem of 'sticks and stones may break my bones, but words will never hurt me'. Back in the day, a boy who cried was labelled 'a big girl' (sorry, ladies!). It was regarded as a betrayal of their masculinity.

The thing is that coping with loss is about working with our emotions. And while the inability to recognise and engage constructively with our emotions at times of loss clearly isn't just a 'man thing', a person's failure to handle their emotions can be deeply destructive, turning sometimes either to violence triggered by anger, or addictions triggered by loss and helplessness. And this is where relationships are so fundamental. Men's tendency to share activities with family and friends, rather than emotions, is not good preparation for bereavement. Women's tendency to share emotions and talk stuff out is far healthier grounding for experiencing loss of any kind.

None of this is to suggest that a woman's deep pain in loss is any less or any greater than a man's pain. Or vice versa. It suggests, however, that the risk of suppressing important emotions in loss is likely to be greater

---

98 Ronald Riggio, *Psychology Today*, 9 October 2014, www.psychologytoday.com/gb/blog/cutting-edge-leadership/201410/how-are-men-s-friendships-different-women-s (accessed 15.12.23).

in men than in women. The lack of a language and cultural conditioning to deal with loss simply compounds the problem.

Getting blind drunk or kicking the cat doesn't deal with anything. It just numbs the pain or hurts the cat.

Conflicting emotions like anger, shame, guilt, shock, envy, relief, denial, regret, vulnerability, numbness, bitterness, anxiety, fear, loss of control, insecurity and abandonment can all kick off and make us feel we're going mad, feeling depressed, suicidal, meaningless, impotent to act or change anything, when what's really happening may all be perfectly normal and part of the grieving process for men, women, children, older people, introverts and extroverts alike, plus any other category of humanity you care to name. But if we don't let anyone in to help us manage what's going on, and we don't have any life preparation for it, how would we know?

Suffering in silence is not the answer. 'Just stay strong for the family' is not the answer for women, just as 'real men don't cry' is not the answer for men.

You may think the theory is all well and good, but how does it work when the rubber hits the road? How do we cope? Let me give you a raw but real example from Vicky's death.

Because of the pandemic and the lockdown rules in place in spring 2020 in England, there was a gap of more than two months between my last visit with Vicky in her care home and the next time I saw her – when she was in her coffin at the undertakers. Thankfully she died peacefully in the presence of her carers. But I had not been allowed to be with her and nor had anyone from our family. I never got to say goodbye while she was still alive. I never got to hold her hand and tell her I loved her in her last days. And because she died of COVID-19 I couldn't even see her body at the undertakers for ten days after her death until she had been quarantined and 'decontaminated'. However distressing the circumstances, I knew rationally that it all had to be that way, so I closed the issue down in my mind and reasoned that I had processed and dealt with it.

Nine months after Vicky's death, my sister-in-law Clare was diagnosed with terminal cancer. Clare had been given only a short time to live when she was diagnosed in hospital. She was discharged and died two weeks later at home with my eldest brother and their children all having been present in their home. I had tried to be as supportive as possible with regular phone calls and messages just to let the family know I was thinking of them, despite the reality there was nothing I could practically do. When my brother called me to say Clare had died, I wept uncontrollably. Naturally I was deeply saddened to lose my sister-in-law, but the intensity of my meltdown really shocked me.

It was an hour or so before I realised her death had triggered me into remembering Vicky's death and how I never had the chance to be with her, how Vicky had no one from her family with her when she took her dying breath, how alone and abandoned she must have felt, even though she could not have expressed it in words. What I discovered was that I was deeply envious that Clare had her family around her at home when she died, because my family and I had been denied that opportunity to comfort Vicky and say goodbye.

Seriously? Envy at the circumstances of someone else's death? How selfish and uncaring! How egocentric can you get?

And yet that's what it was. I felt awful and I felt guilty that I should have such deeply conflicting emotions. But the key thing is that I was able to reconcile these conflicting emotions because the Bereavement Journey course had taught me that envy was a natural, however irrational, emotional reaction to bereavement.

I knew I felt robbed of being with Vicky in her last weeks and moments, but I had reasoned my feelings away by thinking she could not have been discharged home as an active COVID-19 case, and nor could I visit her because of the lockdown rules that were designed to keep me safe. The thing is that my powers of reason had just kicked the can down the road and my feelings of anger and frustration had now come back, accompanied by a deep sense of envy.

This time I was able to identify what was going on in me and deal with it properly over a couple of days by talking it through and crying together with other family members. Within a week I could tell trusted male and female friends what had happened to me without feeling ashamed or thinking they would think less of me. And I hoped my story would help them in preparation for their inevitable times of loss.

The reality that I was unable to be with Vicky when she died will never go away and will always be part of our story. But naming it and processing it meant it didn't have a hold on me anymore. The resentment I had buried and hadn't even known I was carrying was gone. And I could move on with my life.

Managing my thoughts – choosing to think differently

Another way I stretched my soul was by gaining new knowledge around questions and issues I had never previously explored. I gained a new curiosity about the processes and phenomena of grief. I started listening to grieving people in new ways that meant I could empathise rather than just sympathise in the ways I had done in the past. The most obvious result of that stretch into new knowledge and understanding is what you are reading in this book.

Earlier I have referenced the issue of control, and the importance of recognising the only thing we can truly control is how we think about the things happening around us. Easy to say, but hard to do.

In the early days of Vicky's condition, I had received some great advice pointing me to a book written by a neuro-therapist and neuroscience researcher by the name of Dr Caroline Leaf. The first of her books I read was *Who Switched Off My Brain?*[99] Reading Dr Leaf's theories taught me about the critical connections in our brains between our thoughts, emotions, attitudes and behaviours, and their impact on the health and well-being of our brains and bodies.

My simple summary of the connections is:

- Every thought generates an emotion.
- Every emotion generates an attitude.
- Every attitude generates a behaviour.
- Every behaviour generates a thought.

And so on in a continuing thinking cycle.

If the thought is negative, it creates a vicious cycle of toxic thinking that damages the health of our physical brains, and brain cells die.

If the thought is positive, it creates a virtuous cycle that helps our brains stay healthy and flourish.

---

99 Dr Caroline Leaf, *Who Switched Off My Brain?* (Nashville, TN: Thomas Nelson, 2009).

Prior to this I had believed that our thoughts were part of our rational brain (what the brain boffins designate the left side of the brain) and our emotions belonged in the touchy-feely emotional crevices of our mind, the right side of the brain.

Caroline Leaf's work taught me that our rational thoughts and our emotional reactions are entirely and directly connected. She wrote about what the apostle Paul meant when he wrote to the church in Corinth 'we take every thought captive to make it obedient to Christ' (2 Corinthians 10:5). It taught me that I had a choice as to how to capture and control my thoughts and emotions without denying the reality of my circumstances. In summary, I had a choice about how I thought.

Like a proper sceptic, I thought it sounded too good to be true, so I did a few little thought experiments on myself when I felt down, and sure enough I discovered it worked. For example, one day I was at work happily minding my own business, having a pretty good day. I left my study for a bio-break and noticed a couple of minutes later that my mood had changed, and I was feeling irritable. Nothing had happened (or so I thought), no one had called, no one had interrupted me, I hadn't just received annoying news. I wondered what had happened and decided to try out Caroline Leaf's theory on myself.

I tried to retrace my thoughts of the previous few minutes – and it felt like I had had dozens of thoughts in those few minutes! I reviewed as many as I could until, bingo, I had the ah-ah! moment. I remembered an email popped into my inbox, and I remembered not wanting to open it, so I didn't. Why didn't I want to open it? It wasn't the subject matter of the email heading. It was the sender's name that stopped me opening it. And five minutes later it felt like my day was ruined. I was feeling irritable, and the flow of my work had come to a screeching halt. Yet I hadn't even read the email. All of this tortuous thinking had happened in my head and my head alone.

Seeing the sender's name had triggered a series of unconscious thoughts and emotions that I could not have articulated in the moment of receiving the email, and I only understood once I 'took the thought captive'. Finding the thought that triggered my mood enabled me to unpack the emotions generated by the thought. Articulating the emotions helped me to see my attitude towards the sender. And seeing my attitude helped me understand my behaviour and why I was avoiding opening the email. The thought process even helped me to see how I was justifying my behaviour. I realised I was in the vicious thinking cycle, spiralling ever downwards.

I figured that if this thinking cycle stuff worked, I needed to find some appreciative thoughts about the person in question. And to be honest they weren't that hard to find. I just had to articulate them and bring them to the foreground of my thoughts rather than allowing the negative thoughts to dominate my inner monologue.

Guess what? Within a minute I felt fine. My mood had changed back. I felt calm and in control again. I hadn't denied the reality of all the negative stuff, but I had switched to a positive, virtuous cycle of thoughts and emotions. I was ready to open the email and deal with it constructively. And more importantly, my attitude towards the sender had changed. I had become more appreciative. My behaviour with them changed from that point on, as did our relationship. Taking my thoughts captive really worked – as long as I knew what to do with them next.

It's true. I was what Switchfoot called 'the chance of rain'[100] in my own life. Learning to capture my thoughts and redirect them, regardless of the circumstances, would prove key to looking after myself.

It's important to underline the fact that this does not mean denying the reality of our circumstances and burying them. It is about finding positive meaning. And yes, I hear you say that I just can't understand the perverse horrors that have shaped lives in ways I could not imagine. And yes, I can only narrate through the lens of my own life. But you and I can also draw on the inspirational stories of people who have gone to hell and back in their lives and emerged intact with a meaningful life. Nelson Mandela's life is a classic tale of our times. So is Viktor Frankl's.

In *Man's Search for Meaning*,[101] Frankl found meaning for his life in the utter inhumanity, starvation, degradation and fear in Auschwitz and other Nazi concentration camps. His father, mother, brother and wife died in the camps or the gas chambers. Frankl survived and what kept him alive was his search for meaning during the horror. He took what he observed

---

100 'Stars' written by Jonathan Foreman. Copyright © 2005 Meadowgreen Music Company. Administered by Capital CMG Publishing. All rights reserved.

101 Viktor Frankl, *Man's Search for Meaning* (London: Rider, 2004). First published in German 1946.

and experienced about human behaviour in four concentration camps during three long years in captivity, never knowing from one day to the next whether tomorrow would come.

In Frankl's case, he found meaning in two things: staying alive for a person, his wife. And staying alive for a cause, which was his writing about human psychology under the severest pressures possible. We'll say more about Frankl in Chapter Fifteen about finding meaning.

Changing our thinking is much easier to say than to do. While it sounds simplistic, the first step in changing how we think is to accept responsibility for our thinking. It sounds obvious but no one is responsible for my thinking except me.

Like everyone else my life has been bent, shaped and moulded by the circumstances around me and by my experiences. I accept fully that my life has been privileged in so many ways and may not be typical. But the science of the brain and the stories I have heard, both first- and second-hand, tell me the principles hold true whatever our life experience.

In the circumstances I faced with Vicky's decline, I had to accept that I was the only person who could control my thoughts. I couldn't control anyone else's thoughts, especially Vicky's, but no one else could control mine either. They could impact and affect them, of course, but I was and am the only person able to exercise any control over what goes on in my head. And that was the genius of my clinical psychologist's question 'Why would you want to know?' when I told her I was avoiding planning for the future. In the simplicity of her question, I understood there was nothing my knowledge could do to change the circumstances or the journey we were on. Why worry if I couldn't do anything about it? All I could control would be how to react to what we were facing on a daily, weekly and monthly basis. And to let go of the rest.

This letting go of the need to know didn't reduce the pain of our loss, but it did reduce the stress of thinking in any way that I could be in control.

Staying mentally active

Another critical element of my thought life was my professional career.

My work was more than my job to me. It gave me a sense of purpose and meaning in life. My work stimulated me and kept me learning new things with new people and new ideas. I could face the idea of changing the way I worked, I could face the idea of giving up my company directorship. But I couldn't face the idea of not working at all.

We all know the old adage of never regretting time we missed in the office on our deathbeds, but I enjoyed my work because I genuinely thought it made a difference to other people's lives. Even though it helped me escape some of the painful reality of Vicky's decline, it was much more than escapism for me. It was meaningful work and gave me a sense of meaning. It had the by-product of my having to let Vicky get on with her life as best she could, for as long as she could, in a safe environment where I was given the flexibility by my company colleagues to fit my work around her routines and needs. I was very fortunate to be working in a small company where my colleagues were more like family than co-workers, and I could not have got through the journey with Vicky without their love and support.

I had been with the company seven years when Vicky was diagnosed with dementia, and as a director I was entitled to take a sabbatical for a couple of months. I did so four months after her diagnosis and that break gave me something to aim for in the short term and hold on to while our new reality sank in. It was also a special time when we could return to our favourite bolthole on the Atlantic coast of Portugal and see some of Vicky's old friends from her youth when she was living in Angola. Meantime, I could use it as dedicated time to finish writing *How on Earth Did That Happen?* It was an essential time for me to adjust to a new reality in my life, take stock, stretch myself mentally, write my first book and still enjoy her company before it faded irrevocably.

Keep on learning

Vicky and I had the pleasure of having been friends with a couple some twenty-five to thirty years our seniors. Philip and Sheila had always been an inspiration to us in how they stayed young well into their older age. In our church life group, they would tell stories of their childhoods or adult wartime experiences, but never presented themselves as anyone special. Philip was an intrepid adventurer who went pot-holing well into his eighties. Sheila played table tennis regularly at the local club into her eighties. There was always a caravan on their front drive for their holidays, and annual attendance at our church Faith Camp. They were both humble and inquisitive, never patronised anyone younger than them, never talked about things being better 'back in the day', and they never stopped engaging fully in life until their race was run.

Their secret was simply to always keep learning or being curious about people and life. They taught us that continuing to learn, knowing the more you know the less you know, was the key to good ageing. Philip died suddenly aged eighty-six, having bought a new caravan and taught canoeing to a group of youngsters on the River Arun only weeks earlier. He lived his life to the full until the day he died. Sheila grieved his death deeply and naturally, but never gave up living, despite losing her husband when she was in her late seventies. She carried on with her love of table tennis at the local club, tending the garden vegetables, hosting church meetings in her house. And when she was diagnosed with terminal cancer, she accepted her race was run, having lived her life as fully as she could. She carried no bitterness at the hand life had dealt her.

Philip and Sheila instilled in us, through the way they lived, the mindset of being constantly open to new learning about life and all its mysteries. Their simple and down-to-earth humility, with their life-stories through the Second World War years (including Philip's time as a prisoner of war) kept them young at heart through and because of their 'teachability' and openness to new learning. They were open to having their minds stretched throughout their lives.

The process of losing my wife, first to dementia and then to death, opened up perspectives on life that stretched me unbearably on multiple occasions. I think I coped with the stretch because I let myself feel the pain and didn't bury it, but I also needed to learn and understand what was happening to me as much as I learned and understood what was happening to Vicky. That was a key part of taking care of myself and I believe has equipped me to come through my grieving as a more complete human being, but also prepared me to deal with the further losses that are part of life's rich if painful tapestry.

I know that I now respond differently and more healthily to loss than in the earlier years of my life. I now have some language for loss, and I am able more readily to recognise the emotional stuff going on in me, to allow myself to feel sad or a bit blue and pin down why it's happening. I now know that if I have a 'blue day' it won't last forever. I know that if I have a meltdown for half an hour or so it will pass, and I will feel better for it, cleansed and relieved.

I so wish I had understood these things earlier in my life so I could have handled my disappointments and losses as chances to learn about myself rather than embarrassing failures to hide. But I'm thankful it's never too late.

I learned the hard way that personal vulnerability is a strength and not a weakness in men. There's a big difference between admitting things are not going well and indulging in pity parties. Thankfully, the historically macho cultures of the Armed Forces and Emergency Services in the UK now recognise the importance of good mental health, as have world-class athletes such as Simone Biles at the 2020 Olympics (held in 2021, of course, because of the pandemic) and Naomi Osaka the (at the time) four times winner in the Tennis Majors when she withdrew from a tournament in 2021.

It's no longer shameful for a man to cry in public. Rory McIlroy, one of the world's great golfers, wept during his televised interview following Europe's crushing defeat in the Ryder Cup in 2021. No one thought any the less of him. Indeed, it was taken as a public display of how much he cared and was hurting at the loss.

I say I learned the hard way about vulnerability as a strength not because anyone took advantage of my vulnerability, but because I would far rather not have experienced the loss I so grieved in the first place. It was a big price to pay for the learning. The thing with personal vulnerability is that it shows our humanity. It connects and bonds us as human beings. There's something generous triggered in our souls when the vulnerability is genuine.

Have you noticed how much we appreciate leaders who show their humanity and authenticity? While we are less ready to forgive serial errors of judgement from leaders, we are ready to forgive those who admit they got something wrong despite their best efforts, and conversely judge them unfavourably when they pass the buck and blame others or circumstances beyond their control. We like leaders who take genuine responsibility for their decisions, even if we don't agree with those same decisions.

Stretching the spirit

The thing is that grievous loss, in whatever form it comes, makes us either dig deep into the meaning of life and what we believe – or it makes us plough on and tough it all out, burying our heads in the sand and avoiding the uncomfortable questions posed by the acknowledgement of our own mortality.

The simply human standpoint could only take me so far, however, on the journey of losing my wife prematurely to a horrendous degenerative condition. The situation hurt like stink. You might think that a loving God would surely heal her and spare us all the pain we went through as a family. How could a loving God allow this to happen? How do we get our heads around that?

If I had looked after my body and my soul but paid no attention to my spirit, then my care of myself would have been incomplete. My faith gave me anchors to prevent me being blown away by the wind and waves of life.

When Vicky was alive, a relative asked me what her condition had done to my faith. My honest answer was that it had been strengthened and not diminished. I know that has not been every Christian's experience, and I know of many Christians who have been angry with God as a result of what has happened to them. The irony, of course, is they couldn't have been angry with God if they believed he did not exist.

The point I want to emphasise here is that bereavement and grievous loss lead to a deep questioning about our human nature that cannot ever be satisfied by pure reason. And that is the realm of our spiritual work, the realm that takes us into the big uncertainties of life.

Derek Prince wrote in *The End of Life's Journey*: 'Any philosophy or religion that does not have a positive answer to the reality of death is inadequate to meet the needs of humanity.'[102] It's here we face a choice. We can fall back on the *Hitchhiker's Guide to the Galaxy*[103] answer to the Ultimate Question of Life, the Universe, and Everything, which is 42 and took the supercomputer Deep Thought 7.5 million years to calculate. But that isn't a very satisfying way to find the answer if you haven't got 7.5 million years to

---

102 Derek Prince, *The End of Life's Journey* (Fort Lauderdale, FL: Derek Prince Ministries, 2004), p. 10.

103 Douglas Adams, *The Hitchhiker's Guide to the Galaxy* (London: Pan Books, 1979).

spare. Or we can engage with the uncomfortable mysteries of our existence and our mortality through an honest examination of our faith, the beliefs that give us those anchors to guide how we see and think about life, and what we believe about life and death. Those anchor beliefs helped me find meaning in what was happening, but having those beliefs was not enough by itself. In the same way as I had to pay attention every day to exercising my body and my mind, I had to pay attention to my spiritual life every day through a discipline of prayer and quiet meditation on the Bible.

I want to highlight three kinds of spiritual stretch I experienced.

The first is how loss affects our faith. The experience of grievous and painful loss has the effect for some people of confirming their spiritual world-view, and for others of tipping it upside down or destroying it completely.

It takes genuine adversity and loss to find out who we truly are, to test our character. It hurts like hell, it's stressful and it feels cruel. It ruins our appetites and our sleep patterns. It is physically and emotionally exhausting. But it is also necessary in the formation of our character.

In loss some people find God, some others lose the God they thought they knew. Others stay in an agnostic or atheistic worldview that life really is the random chance event they always thought it to be, and that faith is simply a crutch for those unable to accept the reality of random pain and loss. For them, the very experience of loss and unbearable pain seems contrary to any sense of divine justice or love. What's the point of faith when we experience so much pain in life anyway?

In my case, the whole experience of losing Vicky over a period of years stretched my faith to the point of genuinely strengthening it. I wasn't angry with God. I was grateful Vicky and I had enjoyed our life together. I realised there was no point at which the tenets of my faith had promised me an easy ride through life. After all, why would I need faith to get me through the hunky-dory times when life was a bed of roses? On the contrary, it was at the very points of my pain and suffering that my faith anchored my life and gave me a deeper sense of what it means to be alive.

My worldview was never a crutch to lean on when I was limping and the going got tough. If it was a crutch, my muscles would simply have wasted away. It was more like one of those seemingly merciless rehabilitation specialists who get you back on your feet and make you walk and exercise your muscles when all you want to do is sit and curl up in the corner.

Appreciating that my pain was part of my growth as a human being, and not resisting it, was my first spiritual stretch. The second was to exercise and grow my spiritual muscles, not to neglect them.

How did I do that? You may have gathered through my liberal use of musical quotations that I love music. I found in my grief that 'Music has charms to soothe a savage breast'.[104] I surrounded myself with music, much as I had in my teenage years. As I said earlier, I carried a Bluetooth speaker around with me from room to room, or wore my headphones and played a kind of worship music I loved that felt like it kept me connected to God. I would fall asleep every night for months on end after Vicky died with worship music playing softly in the background, like a child's lullaby.

At the same time, as I have mentioned, I found that if I played the kind of blues music I loved, stuff that matched my mood, it would actually take me deeper into my blue mood and sense of abandonment, and that was not a good place to be and would often lead me to find solace in a bottle of red wine. I learned I had to be intentional about the music I played if I wanted to keep some sense of personal equilibrium and not give up on life, especially in the period of intense grief and mourning of the immediate months after Vicky's death.

Ironically, my ability to listen again to some of my favourite blues artists without triggering an emotional meltdown was a sign I was through the intense period of grief. Certain songs would still trigger emotional reactions, but they became more of bittersweet sadness than verging on depression. And I learned that if I felt myself tipping into a 'blue mood' with a song, I would simply stop it and find something more upbeat. I wasn't trying to avoid my natural sadness, but I wasn't going to indulge it either. I had to guard against it taking a hold of me and shaping my identity, shaping who and how I was. Back to that point about choice again. I had a choice whether to indulge my sadness or help myself out of it. And mostly I chose to help myself out of it where I could.

And what about the third thing? I have intentionally saved the best until last.

---

104 William Congreve, *The Mourning Bride*, tragedy in five acts, 1697.

The third thing was recognising Jesus as my source of *shalom*. Back to John 16:33, where Jesus is speaking to his disciples and warns them of the persecution and pain they were about to experience at his death, but that their grief would turn to joy:

> I have told you these things, so that in me you may have peace. In this world you will have trouble. But take heart! I have overcome the world.

Knowing too that I could go to the throne of God with my petitions, 'with thanksgiving', and access 'the peace of God, which transcends all understanding' (Philippians 4:6-7)[105] was a regular source of peace regardless of our circumstances, especially at night when the loneliness felt most acute.

I love the way Jesus never sugar-coated life for us, but promised to give us rest in our troubles:

> Come to me, all you who are weary and burdened, and I will give you rest. Take my yoke upon you and learn from me, for I am gentle and humble in heart, and you will find rest for your souls. For my yoke is easy and my burden is light.
> (Matthew 11:28-30)

Knowing Jesus as my source of peace wasn't the icing on the cake. It was my daily bread, my constant nourishment and source of life.

This taking care of ourselves to take care of others doesn't happen by default. It takes investment. Taking care of my body, mind and spirit took constant effort, discipline, application and effort on my part. The personal toll on my life of caring for Vicky would have been so much greater if I had not invested in myself to do so.

Bad stuff happens to all of us, whether we think we deserve it or not. It's just life, and part of being human. It isn't what happens, but how we react to what happens that shapes the rest of our lives.

---

105 The full quote is: 'Do not be anxious about anything, but in every situation, by prayer and petition, with thanksgiving, present your requests to God. And the peace of God, which transcends all understanding, will guard your hearts and your minds in Christ Jesus.'

Time to reflect

Like the best jazz trios, keeping our personal ensemble in time and sync takes practice and discipline.

Let's pause for thought again, and here are some prompts for you to think about:

- Have you ever had that experience where your loss led you to feel in conflict with yourself?
- You know what to do for your personal well-being, but you just can't find the time or the energy to do it. What is your motivation? Why do you need to look after yourself?
- Have you ever questioned, like I did, why you should be the exception to the rest of humanity and bad stuff should not happen to you?
- Have you let anyone in to listen to your losses? Or do you think they would think less of you if you did?
- Do you want to embrace your loss and allow it to influence how you can live life again with renewed meaning?

Your choice.

Chapter Fourteen: If You Want to Help

After Vicky's death, my grief radar went to a much higher frequency. By that I mean that I became able to engage more explicitly and easily with people who had suffered losses. Losing my wife gave me a legitimacy to ask deeper questions of friends and family. I came to understand that deep grief can be triggered by all sorts of permanent losses, including divorce, a job, a home, a career or a relationship as just a few examples.

I started hearing stories of how well-intentioned people can say and do insensitive and unthinking things because they didn't know what to do or how to speak to people experiencing bereavement or some other kind of grievous loss. They lacked the empathetic language for loss and bereavement. They were never taught or trained to deal with it and defaulted to either avoiding the subject or dealing with it clumsily.

How can we do better and learn the right language? How can we comfort the grieving?

To start, we must try to put ourselves in the place of the bereaved, even if we have never experienced deep loss and grief ourselves.

It sounds really hard. How can we show true empathy when we haven't learned the language of loss?

Kessler offers a simple but profound answer: 'The need is for someone to be fully present to the magnitude of their loss without trying to point out the silver lining.'[106]

Our presence only needs to be just that. Our full presence.

It doesn't demand wise words or inspired counsel. It just requires us to be fully present. No distractions. Fully present. Not looking at our phones, the clock or our watches. Fully present. Not looking around the

---

106 Kessler, *Finding Meaning*, p. 29.

room for help. Fully present. Direct eye contact. Fully present. Physical touch, however light. Fully present.

From all the stuff I've experienced, read, seen and heard, it boils down to three simple things every human being needs in the early and most intense period of grief. They are to be safe, seen and heard. They were certainly what I needed.

Let's unpack them one at a time.

Safe

Feeling safe is fundamental to our mental and physical welfare and well-being. It affects our confidence and our outlook on the world. It helps shape our relationships with other people.

Our relationships with family members are particularly crucial. Our trust in them and reliance upon them to love us and bail us out in times of need is a fundamental support for our sense of personal safety.

Just imagine yourself at home for a moment. Your home's security, strength and ability to withstand shocks depends on the supporting structures. The foundations, the walls, the lintels, the materials, the wiring, the lighting, the alarms, the plumbing and more. We feel secure and safe in familiar surroundings. We check the doors and windows are locked and closed at night if they are in any way accessible to an outsider. We can navigate in the dark, knowing where everything is – or at least where you think you left it last time. It feels great to come back when we've been away. Home sweet home. It may not be the fanciest or the biggest. But it's ours. It's somewhere we can lay our heads and rest.

Then one morning we wake up and someone has removed the doors and windows without asking our permission. They just leave open spaces for anyone to come through any time of day or night. How do we feel now?

Suddenly we don't feel so safe. We feel deeply anxious and vulnerable. The slightest strange sound freaks us out. We dare not leave the house, even though it is wide open. Our sleep is disturbed, and we never feel rested until the doors and windows are back in place.

That's something of what it's like to lose someone who is a fundamental part of us, a touchstone for our personal sense of safety. It is all about our emotions and what we feel. Reason and intellect left the building along with the doors and windows. They are nowhere to be heard or seen.

Imagine that and you're starting to get close to their experience. Reasoning will not touch it. It's how the grieving are feeling that counts.

The big problem with the analogy, of course, is that doors and windows can be replaced, like for like. Loved ones cannot be replaced in the same way.

Our daughter Sam described this period to me after Vicky's death as like having way too many programmes open on her laptop and the wheel of doom just kept spinning around in overload and never processing anything, just stuck in a never-ending cycle and she felt helpless to do anything.

This period of intense grieving does pass, but the loss never leaves us. We can grow through the loss, and we can recover over time, we can install new doors and windows to make us feel safe again, but they will be different doors and windows next time around. More than likely, they will be reinforced and double-lockable for added protection.

Note that I say we *can* rather than we will. We can and will grow if we choose life for ourselves. We won't if we choose to linger on the death. We can and will grow through the loss if we choose to accept and process the reality of our loss emotionally, rationally and spiritually. I had to pay attention to all three: my emotions, my reason and my spirituality to find meaning and hope for the future.

My emotions at the time of Vicky's death made me feel enormously vulnerable. In that intense period of the weeks and months of grief and mourning after her death, I would only share my feelings with people who made me feel safe.

What do I mean by that? They were the people who would not think less of me if I wept or couldn't string a sentence together. They were the people who listened and never left the conversation before I did. They were people who never told me it was going to be OK, that I would get through it, that I should be thankful that I had enjoyed a long and loving marriage with a wonderful woman. They never mocked me, never delved, never competed with me through their stories, never exploited me in any way, never told me to pull myself together, never said I would get over it, never told me their own stories and experiences unless I asked. They gave me advice only when I asked for it. They protected me.

I was fortunate to have a wide circle of family and friends. I was fortunate to have a set of work colleagues who truly cared for my welfare and covered for me at any time when the journey was so hard to bear that I couldn't work.

I don't know how I could have got through the whole journey of Vicky's gradual decline and ultimate death without that circle of relationships around me. And there's the rub, I believe, for many of us – the quality of our relationships. Where do we go for that sense of safety if we have no family or friends to be real with? And that's a key to this issue of emotional well-being – we need people who help us feel safe, that no matter what we might say or do, they will be there for us and won't judge us.

It can be the same with our marriages and partnerships, our jobs, our houses, our place in society. The doors and windows that kept us safe have been removed and simple reasoning doesn't hack it. No matter the reassurances in the moment, you know that life will never be the same again.

It can be good again, but never the same. It can be a very different kind of good, but only if we make the choice to live out of a new sense of meaning and process the loss without fear that it's going to take us down or take us out.

Seen

In the intense period of grief, it was often impossible to find words to express what I was feeling. In the weeks after Vicky's death, I could barely string together a few words, let alone a coherent sentence, without dissolving in tears.

I could plan what to say and how to act ahead of meeting people or returning a phone call. But the plan would rarely last more than a few seconds before I crumbled. As a result, I had to stop returning calls because I knew what would happen. I chose instead to send brief text or WhatsApp messages. Even then I could barely get through typing a message without weeping again. I found the most gracious messages were from people who told me they were not expecting a reply, but just wanted me to know they were holding me in their thoughts and prayers. I knew they saw me.

I learned from that experience, when engaging with family or friends who had lost loved ones, that I should not expect replies or returned calls from them. It didn't mean they did not appreciate my message. They weren't being rude. It just meant they were too overwhelmed to reply. But I wanted them to know they were seen. That someone was reaching out for them. Cue Snow Patrol: 'Hands just reaching out for hands ... It's so damn simple.'[107]

This brings me back to men. Men tend to hide their losses. Men do not like to wear their losses publicly because it feels like failure. Most men don't like public shows of emotion. It doesn't mean they aren't suffering in their grief, but in the analogy of John Gray, they retreat to their caves. In some cases, they wither and die from broken hearts. In others, they resort to alcohol or drugs to numb the pain until the next day. And the next.

The fact we don't see them or they don't ask for help doesn't mean they are OK and don't need help. All too often men don't know how to ask for help for fear of seeming weak.

In my case, I was fortunate to have a handful of friends reach out to me and take me to the pub every so often over the four-plus years between Vicky's diagnosis of dementia and her death. My friend Chris faithfully came and took me out every couple of weeks for a walk and a pint. He let me talk if I wanted to talk, but more than anything else, he just came to be with me. We became much closer in our friendship over that time than we had ever been before.

I felt seen by friends like that.

So, what can we do practically to provide comfort and help people to feel seen in these circumstances?

Everyone grieves in their own unique way, which means there is no single answer. If you know someone has suffered a bereavement and you haven't seen them around or heard from them for a while, don't just assume they are being cared for by someone else. It's possible they have gone to stay with family or that someone has come to stay with them, and they are getting the support they need. There's a real possibility, however, whether male or female, that they have simply withdrawn into themselves and gone

---

107 'Empress' written by Garret Lee, Paul Wilson, Nathan Connolly, Jonathan Quinn, John McDaid and Gary Lightbody. Copyright © 2018 Universal Music Publishing Bl Ltd. All rights reserved.

into hiding. And the longer they hide, the harder it becomes to re-enter and engage with the world.

A simple note through the door, a text or a call to let them know you have been looking out for them and have been wondering how they are doing can work wonders. It will help them feel they are not alone and are seen and haven't stopped existing in other people's eyes – that someone cares. A knock on the door with a meal is a brilliant way of communicating care, regardless of how well we know someone. And there may not be more than a thank you but no invitation to come in for a cuppa. Don't worry. They aren't being rude or dismissive. They may just be hurting so much they have forgotten how to act sociably because they have lost their bearings in life, their sense of safety. Persevere anyway and message again or take another cake or meal. Offer to pick up some groceries. Offer to mow the lawn or wash the car if you can. They will come out of their shell when they feel it's safe to do so.

And if you get invited in? Don't worry about finding the right words. Notice something about their pictures or books or clues about their lives that isn't too intrusive and ask them some simple questions. What's their favourite meal or hobby, what was/is their line of work, where did they like to go on holiday, have they always driven such and such a car? In the early stages of intense grief, don't worry about silence or a lack of response. Simply being there is making them feel seen and cared for.

Never underestimate the power of your presence with a person who is grieving. Your presence can be worth 1,000 wise words. It shows love and care to someone who may have lost the main source of love and care in their lives.

If we realise the person who is grieving has retreated, it's important to show them they are seen. To be touched gently – hands reaching out for hands – either literally or metaphorically. Or hugged firmly, depending on your relationship. I remember the Sunday after my dad died that I went to church and one of the senior pastors saw me and just walked towards me with arms wide open, and gave me a big bear hug and let me cry on his shoulder. He didn't say a word. He didn't need to. I felt genuinely loved and seen.

That's all it takes. Authentic human touch. And eye-to-eye contact.

Or do something kind that shows that you see us. Cook a meal and bring it over, but don't insist we come for a meal. Turn up on the doorstep with some flowers. By the way, blokes like flowers too even if they don't all admit it – at least this one does, and I admit it!

Don't run away or be in a rush. Stay for just a minute unless you feel invited to stay longer because we want to talk.

Heard

When I was still in the intense period of grief but managing to be a bit more articulate and could string a sentence together without breaking down, I wanted to be heard. I didn't want to be asked deep questions or quizzed or probed for detail. But I was OK being asked how I was doing or how I was feeling that day. How was I getting on? I valued being told someone was there for a chat if ever I felt the need, but I didn't want to be pressed to talk. I didn't want to be told not to feel whatever I was feeling. I didn't want to be told Vicky had been released from her pain – I knew that already.

The thing is that so many different emotions kick off at times of grief. If you are feeling angry, the last thing you want to be told is not to feel angry. It doesn't help. And yet you want your anger to be heard and acknowledged. How do you do that? Maybe something like 'it's OK to feel angry' or 'it's natural to feel angry in your circumstances'. Those kinds of statement can offer acknowledgement and some affirmation that we've been heard. It doesn't help if the anger is met by silence. The acknowledgement can also help put a brake on the anger getting out of control by recognising someone is *feeling* angry rather than *being* angry. There is a big difference between a normal person feeling angry and being an angry person.

We don't want to be judged and we don't want to be told to pull our socks up. I didn't need someone to trot out any platitudes or tell me it was time to move on, that time would heal my pain, that 'you and Vicky had a great life together', that I was so blessed to have had a great marriage, to have had such a wonderful family and life together. I both knew and appreciated that stuff and didn't need to be told. I did, however, really appreciate hearing how much Vicky had meant to them, and that joined us together in a kind of shared grief.

Everyone is different. In my case, I didn't want advice unless I asked for it. Other people might find specific advice really helpful but want it to be offered first before it's given. Others might be aching for advice from someone who has been through a similar journey, but are afraid to ask or don't even know what their questions are because they have never been here before. Or their questions might come totally from left field and be completely unexpected.

How do we help in such scenarios, when people's needs can be so complicated and completely different from person to person? A good question may be something like: 'I guess you must have a lot of tricky questions right now. Are there any I can help you with?'

I remember the biggest question I needed answering on the day of Vicky's funeral was simply: 'How long do I wear my wedding ring for?' I didn't know if there were any rules or social expectations. Formally I was now a widower, but in my emotions and mind I still had a wife. How long was an appropriate and respectful period to continue wearing the ring she gave me in our marriage promise? I didn't think to Google the question – that would have been far too rational for my state of mind then. So in the afternoon after the funeral, I plucked up the courage to ask my sister-in-law, who had lost her husband (Vicky's eldest brother) some twenty years earlier and no longer wore her wedding ring. She replied that she didn't actually remember, but thought it was about two years after his death. It wasn't a planned thing, an anniversary of his death, a birthday or anything like that. It wasn't a signal to the world that she was ready for a new relationship – she had a job and four young children at home to raise, so the possibility or desire for a serious relationship never occurred to her. One day she simply thought it was right to take it off. It was that simple.

I had a conversation a month or so later with a friend on the same subject, and his reply was that his mum had always worn her wedding ring, despite his dad dying many years earlier. He could never imagine her taking it off. And they were the kind of stories I found so helpful. They weren't advice as such, but stories of how other people had dealt with the same question. They helped me formulate my own response.

I was always one of those irritating people who would fiddle with my wedding ring, or annoyingly use it to tap out the drumming rhythm of a song on a hard surface – ask my kids, I used to do it all the time on the gearstick in the car to whatever music was playing. It was tight on my finger, so I decided to avoid overcomplicating the matter and wait for a day when it slipped off my finger easily, without having to force it over the knuckle, and when it felt right to leave it off and not put it back on.

The day came about fifteen months after Vicky died, when I was sitting in the car at traffic lights after an evening out with some friends. The lights had just turned red and I started to fiddle with the ring and it slipped off really easily. It had happened before, but this time I knew instinctively I didn't want to put it back on my ring finger. I slipped it on my index finger for safety to make sure I didn't lose it, thinking maybe I could wear it on a different finger from then on.

And that provoked my next question. So, what do I do with it now? I had heard lots of ideas, like wearing it on my right hand or my left-hand index finger, or wearing it on a neck chain, or fusing it with Vicky's ring to wear on a neck chain. But when I got home that evening, I found all my other fingers were either too big or too small to wear it. And I wasn't one for wearing male jewellery other than my wedding ring, so just couldn't imagine wearing a neck chain with it on. I simply put it with Vicky's ring in her old jewellery box, and there it has remained. Both my sister-in-law and friend were right – but I needed to hear it from them, not from a book or an impersonal website.

Reasoning with us doesn't scratch where we are itching when we are grieving. We don't need reason. We need empathy. We need listening to, even when we are making no sense whatsoever. When I was making no sense whatsoever, it was useless telling me I was making no sense whatsoever. I knew that already, but I just needed permission to make no sense whatsoever with whoever was listening.

Remember it's not about you. By all means, offer comfort from how you may have felt the same in your loss, and what the grieving person is going through is normal in grief and mourning. But whatever you do, be careful not to process your own grief from a loss. The bereaved person is not there to comfort you. They are the ones who have experienced the loss. The bereaved don't need your loss to be piled up on top of theirs or feel they have to start comforting you.

While that may sound harsh, the reality is that someone's grief may well trigger historical grief of our own that is unresolved. If that is the case, please notice what is going on in yourself and park it until you have the chance to process it. Don't leave it unresolved but do leave it for later.

There came a time after Vicky's death when I could engage in an intelligent conversation about my loss, but it took a while and it had to be when I felt ready. I now recognise it was a sign that I was coming out of the intense stage of grief. I hadn't stopped grieving, but the period of intense mourning was coming to a close.

What to avoid

Death is the ultimate leveller in life. I don't believe any but the most cold-hearted of people deliberately set out to cause harm to the bereaved. And yet so much harm can be caused by insensitive things said, done or not done, however well-intentioned.

In the previous section I focused on how to help the bereaved in the intense period of their grief. Here I am going to say something about what to avoid.

While there are no hard and fast rules on how people grieve and how to comfort them, simply because every human being is different, there are some obvious things to avoid. In many respects the things to avoid are the opposites of making someone feel safe, seen and heard. I have experienced some of them and I've heard some from other bereaved people. They are simple examples and not exhaustive. Some from family, some from friends, some from neighbours, none of them wilful and many aiming to be helpful but having the opposite effect. Like asking a newly bereaved person when they will be going back to work. Like asking someone if you would like to go out for a coffee 'but we don't have to talk about your dad's death', as if that wasn't precisely the most important thing in their life at that time. Well-intentioned but producing the opposite to the desired effect, with the grieving person feeling unheard and unable to tell their truth.

How about crossing the road to avoid them because you just don't know what to say or do (by the way, I am speaking to myself in the 'you')? Or you are on the other side of the road already and blank them, pretending you haven't seen them. They're both sure-fire ways to make someone feel unseen, unimportant or too hard to engage with. It may be because you genuinely don't have time and are rushing to catch a train or pick up the kids from school. There can be all sorts of legitimate reasons, but the result is to communicate that you don't care, that their loss doesn't matter to you. Try instead to cross the road over to them if you can, and if you really don't have time, just be honest and say you are so sorry for their loss, explain why you're in a hurry and you would really like to give them a call if they are OK with that. It need only take a few seconds. But the result is they feel seen. They are not invisible to you. You care. And please follow up with any promise you make.

I remember a friend I hadn't seen for ages or been in touch with. I was waiting on the corner of a road to cross when she turned the corner in her car and jammed on the brakes when she saw me. Fortunately, there was no traffic behind her, but she stopped her car at the kerb and instantly got out. The mere look in her eyes told me she knew about Vicky, and she stopped her journey to tell me how sorry she was. She couldn't stay long parked where she was, but I knew she cared, and I knew I was seen.

Not knowing what to say or do means some people stay silent and out of touch for fear of upsetting the bereaved person. It may even be because they are grieving the loss themselves and don't want to add to the pain. Or they assume lots of other people may be filling the space – and that's a dangerous assumption if everyone is thinking the same. It compounds the high likelihood that the bereaved person themselves will not be in a place to reach out. If they're anything like me, where I couldn't string two sentences together to ask for help at the height of my grief, or even know what help I needed, this assumption that other people are filling the space can lead to the prospect of isolation and feeling of rejection.

If you don't know what to say or do, and maybe dread the painful silences or tears in a conversation, think instead to send a simple text message to remind them you are thinking of them. It only takes a few seconds and you don't have to enter an awkward conversation. Those few seconds of effort people took to send me a simple message really helped me feel seen and supported. It's not difficult. Don't expect a reply necessarily but know your message has been appreciated. Like Snow Patrol say – it's so damn simple!

My daughter Sam and I both had experiences of people ringing us a few weeks after Vicky's death to express their condolences in phone calls that turned into 'by the way' conversations that left us both feeling they only got in touch because they wanted something from us. Those calls made us feel the condolences were empty pretexts to ask something of us and were not genuine.

Does that mean you can't ask anything of someone in grief? Not at all. In fact, they might well appreciate the distraction or the knowledge their help can still be of value. It's about having the sensitivity not to ask for something while making contact for the first time since their loss. Keep the messages separate. You wouldn't send someone a birthday card and ask them for a loan in the same card, so why offer someone condolences and then ask them for a favour in the same call?

Another friend whose mother died suddenly when living abroad could only just get there in time with her husband for the day of the funeral. After they returned home, and still in a state of shock, she was asked, 'Are you OK?' It was a well-intentioned and seemingly inoffensive question, but for my friend it was inappropriate and only had one possible answer. How could she possibly be OK in such dreadful circumstances? How could these be the first words of the first communication uttered by a friend? The seemingly innocuous question 'Are you OK?' displayed little insight into her grief, and yet was meant with concern and love. It is precisely the kind of question that can be asked by people of good and caring intent yet lack the language for death and grief. Yes, it can be a tightrope to tread delicately, but it is a tightrope we can learn to cross with a bit of conditioning and practice.

What can you say in such circumstances if a simple question like 'Are you OK?' triggers an angry reaction? The reality is that everyone is different and reactions will vary. A massive amount depends on the nature of the loss and the nature of your relationship. In my case, it helped to keep it simple. Something like, 'I'm so sorry for your loss. I just can't imagine how you are feeling.' Or maybe, 'Is there any way I can help right now?' – but only if you genuinely mean to follow it up.

This is all tough territory to navigate, but if you remember to see the person in front of you and acknowledge what they are feeling, you will be on the right track. In my case, I didn't find statements like 'Vicky is at peace now', that were meant to comfort me, as helpful at all because they were statements about Vicky when I was the one grieving and in deep pain. I knew she was at peace, but I was the one in pain and needing to be heard and seen. Instead, maybe let the bereaved person know what the deceased meant to you – the things that touched me most were when people told me what Vicky meant to them or how she had influenced their lives. Or how much they missed her too.

Stay in touch – don't withdraw altogether

The previous sections have been mainly about supporting people through the initial and most intense period of grief. And while it was not my own experience, I have heard stories from people who felt well supported at the time of deepest crisis, but then found the support melted away after the initial and most intense period. They felt seen and heard for a while, but then forgotten as life 'returned to normal'.

It is important to recognise that life seldom if ever returns 'to normal' for the person working their way through grief. The need to be safe, seen and heard is a constant human requirement and doesn't fade even as the loss starts to retreat in memory and time.

I was (and am) very fortunate that the people closest to me during the most intense period of loss, and indeed during the journey with Vicky's dementia, stayed close and didn't melt into the background. Some of the ways we stayed in regular touch were initiated by them and some by me. They didn't leave it all up to me and I didn't leave it all up to them. A year after Vicky's death they would still check in on how I was doing, and while our conversations reflected how life had moved on, her death was never a taboo subject. Those people weren't necessarily in my life week in, week out. With some friends it was every couple of months, with others every week or couple of weeks.

The point to emphasise here is that the quality of our relationship was based on more than the episode of Vicky's death. The episode of Vicky's death served to take the relationships to a greater depth and durability. It took our relationships to a higher level of trust for having gone through the furnace of vulnerability and deep humanity. I felt safe in my vulnerability and deeper in our relationships. Nothing was off the agenda anymore in those friendships.

I remember how my parents, having lived through the Second World War years with their army comrades and friends, never missed an annual reunion of dad's tank regiment, and had lifelong friendships forged in adversity. My experience of losing Vicky could never be compared to the sacrifices and horrors of war they experienced together, but I think you get my drift that true friendships are shaped in the tough times of life. And unless we can let people into our adversity, our friendships will never flourish.

The more vulnerable I was with my family and friends, the more vulnerable they became with me about their own lives and concerns. They weren't pity parties or calls for attention, but our conversations took on a new quality and ease for dealing with a subject of such ultimate concern, like death. We stopped scratching the polite surface of British culture and life and went to places in conversations that we had never been before. Don't get me wrong, it wasn't all deep and meaningful stuff – we could share fun and have a laugh too.

Building on what we have already written about men, the key point to communicate here is the importance of sustaining for the long run the relationships we develop in times of loss. So much of this is about drawing men back and out into the wider community where they can offer their experience, talents and skills and re-establish their sense of self-worth.

Naturally, the same principles apply to women. If a retired builder can volunteer their skills to develop, decorate or refurbish a community facility, if a retired artist or dancer can teach their skills to local children or other adults, if a retired bus driver can drive the community minibus to take the elderly shopping, if a retired accountant can keep the books and accounts of a bunch of local charities, if a retired lawyer can offer their expertise to support single-parent families in legal difficulties, if a retired banker can run a debt-recovery programme to families in debt, all these things have a double whammy, a win-win for the individual and the community in which they live. They can all give a new sense of purpose and value to men and women struggling to recover from bereavement and find fresh meaning and self-worth in life.

Time for reflection

It's time to pause again. Being alone in times of loss is dangerous for our health, so here are a few more questions to prompt your reflections.

- Have you considered how readily you are able to express your emotions when experiencing loss?
- Who would you talk to about your feelings if you had just lost a loved one, your job, your marriage or your home?
- How wide is your circle of friends and family to help you through those times of loss that happen in life?
- Is there anything you can do to enlarge your circle of friends?

Chapter Fifteen: Hope Springs Eternal

In the year after Vicky's death, I had to find a new rhythm of life. Some of it was based on our shared routines and habits, like going for a walk every day. Other aspects of my day were now my own distinct and personal routines and habits. But regardless of whether they were new routines or old shared routines, they were now entirely my choice. I had to find my own way.

The awakening experience

In *Staring at the Sun*, Irwin Yalom writes about the 'awakening experience'[108] in life. He describes how Ivan Ilych, the protagonist from Tolstoy's *The Death of Ivan Ilych*[109] is a middle-aged, self-absorbed and arrogant bureaucrat who develops a fatal abdominal illness and is dying in unremitting pain:

> As death approaches, Ivan Ilych realises that all his life he has shielded himself from the notion of death through his preoccupation with prestige, appearance and money. He becomes enraged with everyone about him who perpetuates denial and falsity by offering unfounded hopes for recovery.
>
> Then, following an astounding conversation with the deepest part of himself, he awakens in a moment of great clarity to the fact that *he is dying so badly because he has lived so badly*. His whole life has been wrong. In shielding himself from death, he

---

108 Yallom, *Staring at the Sun*, Chapter 3, p. 31.

109 Leo Tolstoy, *The Death of Ivan Ilyich* (Scotts Valley, CA: CreateSpace Independent Publishing Platform, 2011).

has shielded himself from life as well... In short, he becomes *mindful of being.*[110]

Ebenezer Scrooge, in Charles Dickens' *A Christmas Carol*[111] undergoes a similar kind of existential shock therapy, and transforms from a grasping, isolated, mean-spirited man into a warm, generous person eager to help his employees and associates. That's what Yalom calls an 'awakening experience'.

As a psychotherapist, Yalom writes of the many reports of dramatic and lasting changes he witnessed in clients through their confrontation with death:

> Many reported a diminishment of their fears of other people, a greater willingness to take risks, and less concern about rejection. One of my patients commented drolly that 'cancer cures psychoneuroses'. Another said to me, 'What a pity I had to wait till now, till my body was riddled with cancer, to learn how to live.'[112]

Truth be told I can't say I stopped thinking about the *how* of life after Vicky died, and I still haven't, but her death woke up in me an urgency to live the authentic life of engagement and meaning Yalom describes. It was my 'awakening experience'.

Finding meaning

In the immediate months after Vicky's death, I asked a couple of friends, one a professional counsellor and the other a psychotherapist, to recommend some books to help process my grief. The first and most helpful book I read was one I have already referenced many times: *Finding Meaning*

---

110 Yalom, *Staring at the Sun*, p. 35.

111 Charles Dickens, *A Christmas Carol* (Scotts Valley, CA: CreateSpace Independent Publishing Platform, 2011).

112 Yalom, *Staring at the Sun*, p. 34.

by David Kessler. In his introduction to *Finding Meaning*, Kessler wrote: 'Those able to find meaning tend to have a much easier time grieving than those who don't.'[113]

Kessler teaches that pain in grief is inevitable, while suffering is optional. How so? He argues they are not interchangeable because:

> Pain is the pure emotion we feel when someone we love dies. The pain is part of the love. Suffering is the noise our mind makes around that loss, the false stories it tells because it can't conceive of death as random. Death just can't happen. There must be a reason, a fault. The mind looks for where to lay the blame, perhaps on ourselves, perhaps on someone else... Our own version of our loved one's death – the story we tell ourselves about it – can either help us heal or keep us mired in suffering.[114]

Our suffering depends on whether we see the death as meaningful or a cause for blame. In truth, I had little difficulty seeing Vicky's life as meaningful and therefore her legacy as meaningful too. So, while I grieved and mourned her death intensely, I didn't look to blame anyone or anything or create a false story about her death.

Her life had had meaning. But what about mine? Where was my meaning in life now? It really depended on how I chose to react to it. Back to Kessler when he says 'meaning is what *you* make happen.'[115]

The Bereavement Journey course was genuinely transformational for me. It helped me understand what was happening in me and the internal monologues that kept looping around. It helped me name and process the contradictory emotions I had experienced and helped me see myself as normal, and neither going mad, failing or weird. I saw how it set fellow grieving participants free of their guilt and shame.

Before the course was finished, I resolved the first meaningful thing I would do was to offer to run the course for others in my church who I knew had suffered bereavements during that awful period of the

---

113 Kessler, *Finding Meaning*, p. 3.

114 Ibid., p. 51.

115 Ibid., p. 7.

pandemic lockdown in 2020. The response from within the church was humbling and astonishing at the same time. There was an overwhelming gratitude that we were helping people to heal deep wounds in their lives that had been covered with sticking plaster. And it gave birth to a fresh compassion and understanding on how we could support people in loss.

Healing in finding purpose

As a survivor of the Holocaust Victor Frankl wrote his classic *Man's Search for Meaning*. It is a monument to hope in the dreadful and dark times he experienced. Frankl was a professor of neurology and psychiatry at the University of Vienna whose clinical theory of psychotherapy (called logotherapy) was massively influenced by what he saw and experienced first-hand as a prisoner for three years in Auschwitz and three other Nazi concentration camps. His father, mother, brother and wife died in the camps or were sent to the gas ovens. Frankl and his sister were the only ones to survive from their family. He was eminently qualified to write about how to find life worth preserving.

Frankl's theory of logotherapy was his way of creating a pattern of meaning and responsibility from the broken threads of life. When entering Auschwitz, he was stripped naked of all his clothes and belongings, his head and body shaved, his precious manuscript with his life's work destroyed.

In his Preface to *Man's Search for Meaning* Professor Gordon Allport writes that 'Frankl is fond of quoting Nietzsche, "He who has a *why* to live can bear with almost any *how*"'.[116] It is purpose – our personal why? – that gives us meaning in life.

He says the last of human freedoms, when all human dignity has been stripped away, is the ability 'to choose one's attitude in a given set of circumstances'[117]. Everything can be taken from a human being but the ability to choose how we see what we see and experience. Frankl describes it as 'the

---

116 Frankl, *Man's Search for Meaning*, p. 9.

117 Ibid., p. 9.

spiritual freedom that cannot be taken away, that makes life meaningful and purposeful.'[118]

As a psychiatrist, Frankl knew from experience that anyone who lost faith in their future was doomed to die. He wrote:

> Those who know how close the connection is between the state of mind of a man – his courage and hope, or lack of them – and the state of immunity in his body will understand that the sudden loss of hope and courage can have a deadly effect.[119]

Frankl's theory, developed as a result of his learning and experience of 'man's inhumanity to man',[120] boils down to something quite simple:

> The more one forges himself – by giving himself over to a cause to serve or another person to love – the more human he is and the more he actualizes himself.[121]

In summary, Frankl survived three years of inhumane treatment and degradation in four Nazi concentration camps, not knowing from one day to the next whether he would survive each day, because he found two basic sources of meaning:

- A cause to serve – his life's work in psychotherapy.
- People to love – most specifically his wife, whose fate was unknown to him during his imprisonment.

A cause to serve – seeing beyond my circumstances

So much for the theory and inspirational words. What did they do for me? How did my loss 'add meaning' to my life?

---

118 Frankl, *Man's Search for Meaning*, pp. 75-76.

119 Ibid., p. 84.

120 Robert Burns, www.brainyquote.com/quotes/robert_burns_182941 (accessed 4.12.23).

121 Frankl, *Man's Search for Meaning*, p. 115.

I had always believed my life had purpose. I was fortunate to have enjoyed a career full of purposeful work – at least, it was purposeful to me. I was blessed to have deeply loving relationships in my marriage and my family. I had a worldview shaped by my faith.

I know those experiences are not common and are not shared by everyone. I know we are all different and have very differing life experiences. But to focus on the differences in our circumstances would be missing the point.

In 2004, sixteen years before Vicky's death, I had made a significant career change. I had been a chief executive in two NHS trusts for twelve years and had started to run out of the energy and commitment the job required. I had loved the work and felt privileged to serve in such a position, but I found my motivation was diminishing and my heart wasn't in it anymore. I feared I was becoming cynical and losing my love of work, so I decided to step out of it before it changed me into a political 'game player' and I lost my authenticity. I recognised the things I loved about the job were all to do with helping improve people's lives, and I especially loved the feeling of opening up new possibilities for people that they had never seen for themselves.

Three years later I joined a consultancy called Tricordant where we developed a consulting method we called the Golden Cycle, based on Simon Sinek's insights in his book *Start with Why*.[122] The first question in the method, unsurprisingly, was 'What's your Why?', your core purpose, your reason for existence, what gets you out of bed in the morning, what makes your work and life worthwhile? I couldn't use the method, however, without knowing that my own Why, to give my life meaning, was to help people see beyond their daily circumstances so they could live flourishing lives. In that respect, having a sense of purpose in life wasn't something new to me. What was new was to realise I could grow even more in my sense of purpose through and because of my loss.

I didn't have to search too hard to find my sense of meaning sharpened and more clearly focused. I quickly discovered that my grief and loss radar had tuned to a higher frequency than ever before in my life. This loss was beyond my understanding or any previous experience. I decided I had

---

122 Simon Sinek, *Start with Why* (Brentford, UK: Portfolio, 2011).

to understand as much as I could and make some sense of the apparent cruelty of my wife losing her life and mental capacity at the very point she should have been in her prime. I really was not prepared for it, and I had to learn quickly to get through.

Hence my reading and research. Hence my curiosity and conversations with people to find out how they experienced loss and bereavement, and how often people were ill-prepared to handle it when it happened. And how clumsily people around them handled their responses, often with devastating results on the bereaved person and their relationships.

As I have already mentioned, I attended a bereavement course I thought I didn't need (typical bloke response) and found it transformative. I started to understand the deep emotions triggered by loss, how reason flew out the door in the intense period of grief following Vicky's death.

My take on this experience is that I am far from alone. Indeed, my experience is pretty typical. And in that I found a new sense of meaning in an urge to help and support people through their losses – and that's why I decided to write this book.

But writing a book takes ages. It isn't just the writing, it's the editing, the reviewing by friends, finding a publisher and all that. That all takes time. I also had an urge to try to make a difference more immediately to other people's lives. That's why I started running the same bereavement course I had experienced just a few weeks after completing my own and within six months of Vicky's death.

Seeing and hearing the difference the Bereavement Journey course is making to people's lives is enormously rewarding and meaningful. It is not the only resource out there, but it is the one that has made a difference for me and so many others who go on to volunteer to lead and facilitate groups themselves.

People to love

Despite my loss, I still had a loving family with three daughters all with families and children of their own. Our family had changed because Vicky was no longer present physically and practically, and her presence was now in our memories, our hearts and our emotions. I realised that loving our family was now *my* responsibility rather than a shared responsibility with Vicky.

My people to love gave increased meaning to my life.

There was still a big hole in my life, of course, in missing the *one* person to share life with at the most intimate of levels. I no longer had a wife. In a memorable phrase I heard in a bereavement course, I no longer had someone to do nothing with. But I still had a family to love and to love me.

Appreciate life, the living and the dead

Some of the most emotional moments for me in grieving Vicky's death were triggered by reading the tributes written by friends and family in the days after her death, whether by card, text, Facebook message or whatever means. They were all moving reminders of what she meant to people in her life, the impact she had made upon them, the images they treasured of her.

Despite her inner strength, Vicky sadly never had any great sense of confidence in herself. She had always put other people above and before herself, but never had any sense of her own importance to others. She had always tried to encourage other people but would be hard on herself when others tried to encourage her.

Like the friend who wrote to me about Vicky being one of the two most influential women in her life.

Like my sister who described her as 'the kindest, loveliest lady I ever knew'.

More than a year after her death, I was at a meeting in my church when a young woman Vicky had befriended many years earlier approached me. I had only seen her once by chance, when I had broken the news to her that Vicky had died. She approached me on this later occasion to ask how I was and immediately had to choke back her own tears as she told me how much Vicky had meant to her and her young daughter. She had to break off the conversation and walk away to regain her composure. After a few minutes, she came back and apologised for bringing up Vicky's death and how bad she felt for doing so – but I was able to tell her I was glad she had, and genuinely appreciated what she had said because she had told me how much Vicky had meant to her and the difference she had made to their lives as a family. That was far better for me than any platitude about how she would now be at peace or having a party in heaven. It was an authentic appreciation of Vicky's life and legacy.

I truly appreciated those messages. But I also thought how much those same messages would have meant to her *if she had heard or read them when she was alive*. How much they would have let her know her value during her life. And how much difference they might have made to the way she thought about herself, to her self-esteem. And to her mental well-being and health as well. Who knows?

Why do we have to wait until someone dies to let them know how much we appreciate them and what they have meant to us? Why can't we appreciate the living as much as we appreciate the departed? Why do we have to wait for the tributes at the funerals or the obituaries in the papers?

Let's take a leaf out of Joan Armatrading's 'Shapes and Sizes', prompted by the death of the much-loved BBC Radio 4 presenter of the *Today* programme, Brian Redhead:

> It comes all shapes and sizes
> It's something you can never buy
> Don't wait until it's over
> Before you say it's all been fun
> Obituary columns are filled with love.[123]

How about we think about the people who have most influenced us in our lives, in whatever aspect of life and whatever age, and let them know? A kind of prebituary, if you like. Please don't tell me that's not a word. I know. But hopefully you get the point.

Towards incomplete completeness

Here's a weird and paradoxical thought to end this chapter. I'm not sure whether to call this bit complete incompleteness or incomplete completeness.

---

123 'Shapes and Sizes' written by Joan Armatrading. Copyright © 1995 BMG Rights Management. All rights reserved.

In a conversation with a friend over a year and half after Vicky's death, I found myself saying that I now felt more complete as a human being because I had gone through the experience of losing my wife.

However contradictory it sounds, I was also incomplete because of the enormous hole her death had left in my life. No other loss had ever come close to that deep grief or to making my life feel more incomplete without her.

And yet I felt more complete because I had experienced the fullness of both deep joy and deep grief. My spectrum of life experience was more complete than it was before Vicky's death.

I'm more aware now of my incompleteness. I'm more aware than ever that I can never figure everything out or plan how life will turn out. While I can know what happened, I will never understand why Vicky had to lose her mental capacity and life in such a seemingly cruel way. I will never understand why our children and grandchildren never got to see her flourish in the prime of her life and why she was taken away from them in such a painful way. Why torture myself with questions of that kind when I can never know the explanation in this life anyway? Why entertain questions about a past I can no longer influence? What's the point and where's the meaning in that?

Searching for meaning in grievous loss is quite different to searching for explanations about the loss. Explanations about a loss can help with closure and acceptance of a loss. They can help people move on with life. But they don't necessarily give them meaning in their own lives. There is a world of difference between the question 'What caused this to happen?', which is orientated to our past, and the question 'How can I make life more meaningful because of this?', which is orientated to our future and can give us a cause to live for in the present.

Experiencing grievous loss has exposed me to a level of human experience I may have known existed, but I had never *felt*. Maybe my new sense of completeness has something to do with my emotional self beginning to catch up with my rational self. Knowing something exists is very different to experiencing it.

Experiencing grievous loss has opened my eyes to how badly a culture obsessed with success prepares us for the losses we will inevitably experience in life.

I hope and pray that the story of our experience may in some small way help prepare you better for the losses that come your way. I hope it will give you some language, both spoken and emotional, to help others when they suffer loss. That would be very meaningful for me.

When grievous losses happen, you won't be failing. You will be living a fully human life.

Time to reflect

It's that time again to take a pause and reflect for a few minutes with some questions:

- Do you now feel better equipped to help others who suffer loss? If so, how?
- Have you explored the meaning of your losses and what you have learned from them?
- How can you show true appreciation of the people who have most influenced you while they are still alive?

Chapter Sixteen: Working For My Good

And we know that in all things God works for the good of those
who love him …
    (Romans 8:28)

This Bible verse anchored me through the storm of Vicky's dementia, decline
and death. It gave me hope that good would come of my experience of her
decline and death.

My hope

In Chapter Fifteen I wrote about hope springing eternal, and how we can
find meaning in a cause to serve and people to love.

A large part of this book is intentionally focused on the human experience of loss. If we don't pay attention to the human aspects of loss, we will
miss the point of how the love of God speaks deeply into this fundamental
human need to have meaning in life, even in extreme circumstances of
loss. Faith in God gives me a cause to serve and people to love. Is that not
the heart of the Good News and the gospel message?

Having faith doesn't mean we live a fur-lined, well-fed and sugar-coated
life where the necessary stuff drops into our laps just by sending a quick
prayer upstairs.

Why didn't God just change my situation and make it better?

Faith in Christ gave me the tools to navigate the choppy waters and wild
winds of life when they arrived – and they most certainly did – without
going under and drowning. It helped me rise above and overcome the
circumstances I faced. It didn't mean I could avoid the circumstances, and
indeed they didn't change, despite the prayers of many faithful believers,

but I changed in and through the circumstances. I am now both more complete and more incomplete as a result.

Life doesn't always turn out the way we would like it to. But faith is for every situation and the Bible foretells pretty well every situation we might face, both the rough and the smooth (mostly the rough, actually) and the responses we need to persevere and overcome them.

My meaning

Viktor Frankl's book *Man's Search for Meaning* provides incredible evidence of how the human spirit is equipped not only to survive but to overcome the most devastating and dehumanising of experiences *if only* we can find meaning in those circumstances.

The thing is that meaning doesn't just fall off the shelf into our outstretched hands. We have to search for it and be intentional about persevering until we find it. Frankl boiled it down to living for a cause or living for a person, or both.

I find meaning in helping people navigate the tricky waters of how to support people in their losses. What to do, what not to do, what to say and what not to say.

I find meaning in seeing people realise they have not lost the plot when they are behaving in ways they don't normally behave.

I find meaning when I hear people talking about bereavement with understanding of what they or others are experiencing.

I find meaning when people's lives get unstuck because they have been helped to process their losses.

I find meaning in telling the story of Vicky's decline and death so as to honour her life and legacy.

I find meaning in trying to unravel the mystery of why death is a taboo subject in our First World, success-orientated society, despite its inevitability.

I find meaning in challenging the church to engage with the humanity of death, and in encouraging the church to tackle our social epidemic of aversion to loss.

I find meaning in knowing my life has a purpose despite the pain.

In my meaning I found a crown of 'beauty instead of ashes'. I found joy to replace my mourning. I found a 'garment of praise instead of a spirit of despair'.[124]

And I find meaning in sharing this story with you through the writing of this book.

I trust you can find meaning from reading it.

And maybe you can now help others find meaning in the pain of their losses too. Let's write some unwritten[125] chapters together.

Drench yourself in words unspoken.
Live your life with arms wide open.
Today is where your book begins.
The rest is still unwritten.

May the next chapter of your life be the best chapter of your life.

---

124 Isaiah 61:3.

Acknowledgements

I like to think of this book as being crowd-written. My name might be on the cover, but the invisible hands of so many people have been writing with me.

Thank you to those friends and family who have supported and helped me along the way with their encouragement and insights. To name but a few, I want to pay particular thanks to:

- My daughters Ali, Sam and Rachael, for providing their insights into their own loss and engaging with the highly emotional process of reviewing an early draft to check for factual accuracy.
- My senior pastor, Clive Urquhart, for his openness and generosity of spirit to give me the platform publicly to open up this difficult subject in my church following Vicky's death.
- Andrew Boyd, for his constant encouragement to take this book from concept to publication, ploughing his way through the very first draft, providing invaluable critique and constructive advice.
- Tony Larkin, for his encouragement as a professional psychotherapist, providing me with enlightening literature to read along the way and ensuring that I wasn't 'going off on one' in my drafting and references to the psychology of grief and loss.
- Rachel Larkin, for her down-to-earth critique of an early draft. When Rachel tells you something is 'quite good' it is one of the highest compliments a writer could ever receive.
- Joanna Thomas, my co-leader for the Bereavement Journey courses we run, for her critique of the draft and her constant encouragement that what I have to say feels so relevant and necessary.
- Sarah Holloway, for her creativity and imagination in capturing poetically the essence of the book in her cover design.

I also need to thank the numerous friends and family who have contributed stories and examples along the way, sharing their own pain in such open and honest ways to help enrich the insights I have been able to write about. I'm sorry I cannot name you all – but you know who you are, and your contributions have been invaluable.

And of course, to Vicky. This book is just a small part of your legacy.

Made in the USA
Monee, IL
24 June 2024

60420918R00134